Dancing in *Heaven*

a sister's memoir

CHRISTINE M. GROTE

Dancing
in
Heaven

a sister's memoir

Grote Ink, LLC
Cincinnati

Published by Grote Ink, LLC., Cincinnati, Ohio.

ISBN – 13: 978-0-9838198-0-6
ISBN – 10: 0983819807

Edited by Carolyn Walker and Jeffrey S. Hillard
Designed by Anna M. Grote
Illustration by Matthew A. Grote

ACKNOWLEDGMENTS

Amazing Grace by John Newton was one of Annie's favorite church songs. It was played at her funeral at the request of our mother. I am grateful to be able to include the lyrics here.

I would like to thank my readers and editors:

My mother who was brave enough to read this even while still mourning.

My husband Mark who encouraged me to continue.

My good friends Marcia Kluesener and Cathy Steinriede.

Carolyn Walker, workshop mentor, college professor, and memoirist, who edited the early draft of Dancing in Heaven and helped to shape the final story. She read and commented with wisdom, sensitivity and compassion, for which I will be eternally grateful.

Jeffrey S. Hillard, college professor, editor and friend, who encouraged me to keep going and stand by my vision, and who provided copy editing for me.

My creative son and industrial designer, Matthew A. Grote, who understood what I was looking for in a graphic for the cover and provided it for me.

Credit for the final design of this book goes to my talented and generous daughter and graphic designer, Anna M. Grote, who spent many hours, without promise of compensation, designing the layout and cover.

The names of most individuals who are not family members have been changed. Some photographs have been digitally altered.

I would like to take this opportunity to thank the hospice nurses who cared for Annie and our family with tenderness and compassion in this time of great need.

I particularly want to thank my sister Carol who understood what this project has meant to me, who graciously agreed to be part of it, and who held me up when the going got rough.

Finally, I want to thank both of my parents who have supported me throughout the years and who have always believed in me.

CHAPTERS

Amazing Grace, how sweet the sound,
That saved a wretch like me.

I once was lost but now am found,
Was blind, but now I see.

CHAPTER 1 **Watching in the Night**

October 5, 2009

It's 1:45 in the morning and I'm having trouble sleeping again. Vivid scenes from August play unbidden through my mind on an endless loop.

I abandon the effort to sleep and get out of bed to retrieve my robe from the bathroom hook, stopping for a moment to search out the window and into the darkness. I stand motionless watching the night, listening, waiting, hoping. I see only our still front yard and its massive oak tree, the early autumn colors illuminated by the porch light below my window. I hear nothing.

I do a quick calculation in my head. Seven weeks. Almost to the day. Since Annie died.

I tiptoe around the bed to get my glasses from the nightstand, trying not to wake my husband or our seven-month-old, little, white peek-a-poo Arthur.

I surrender to the insistent memories that disrupt my rest and walk downstairs directly to my computer desk. The glow from a light left on in the family room that filters down the hall isn't bright enough to illuminate where I sit. I can't see the keys on the keyboard. Even so, I am reluctant to turn on a light and disturb the darkness.

Arthur is crying upstairs. His radar on my every movement must have issued an alarm. I go back up the stairs, open the door to his cage where he lies beside my bed, pick him up, and return downstairs to take him outside to his fenced-in area.

The silence, solitude and darkness outside bring a tingle to my skin although the air is still warm. Again I stand very still to search and listen—but nothing.

Arthur has finished his business. I pick him up, return inside, and lock the door. I settle him on the folded blanket beside my desk where he often sleeps as I work.

I've known I needed to write this story for a while now. I would tell my sister Annie's story in her own words if I could. In fact, there is nothing I would like better than to tell her story from her perspective. But I don't know what she was thinking or how she felt. It wasn't possible while she was alive and any remote hope that someday, somehow she might be able to communicate that to us has died with her.

I know I need to write this story, but I am afraid I have waited too long and won't be able to remember it clearly. I am afraid it is too soon and I will remember it too well.

CHAPTER 2   **A Part of Me**

Day 1

Friday July 24, 2009

The real fear started with the phone call from Carol.

I'm getting dressed in my bedroom when the phone rings. It's my sister Carol.
One year older than me, Carol is something of a "wanderer" as she would say.
She has lived at my parents' house on and off through recent years where she
has her own room upstairs. She is an artist, an energy healer, and a free spirit.
Although she is one year older than me, she is, and has almost always been,
smaller than me in stature. She is about 5'2", thin, and has a small frame. Her
hair is still a light brown/blonde color, and she has been wearing it long recently,
mostly pulled back in a clip. Her eyes are a vibrant crystal blue. She is vigilant
about her diet of health foods and supplements. She dresses with an artistic flair
and maintains a simple life-style.

Where Carol is creative and artistic, I am logical and have a scientific background.
I used to engage in frequent arguments with her about some of her convictions
and beliefs. Now I admit I don't know everything about the way the world, which

may include the spirit world, works. I accept that some of her beliefs and views may be valid, and I leave it at that.

Carol supports herself through her business that offers transformational healing, inspirational programs, and visionary art. She works from home. As far as I'm concerned, this is a good situation. My parents still live with, and take care of, my sister Annie, who was born with severe brain damage the year after me. She doesn't walk or talk and requires the care of an infant. It gives me a sense of security that Carol is there to help Mom with Annie and, quite frankly, with Dad who was diagnosed with early-stage Alzheimer's right before Christmas last year. Many times Carol will take care of Annie while our parents are out, usually visiting our grandmother who lives about forty-five minutes away.

When I answer the phone I say hello to Carol as I stand looking at my face reflected in the mirror of my dresser. In my mind I go through the litany of criticisms of myself, thinking that I really do need to lose some weight. I contemplate yet again coloring my shoulder length, mostly dark hair to hide the gray. My brown eyes look tired and remind me more of my grandmother's eyes than the bright ones of my three brown-eyed sons.

"I've been thinking about this a lot, and I felt I needed to tell someone," Carol says. "I've been living here, and I see what is going on day after day. I feel like maybe we should be doing something. Annie's really sick."

Carol's words jar me from my self-inspection. "What's going on?" I ask.

"Annie isn't getting over the bronchitis. She hasn't been eating and she looks terrible," Carol says. "She doesn't seem like herself at all."

"In what way?" I ask. "What do you mean?"

"She isn't smiling anymore."

Annie was always generous with her smiles. She loved being around us, and although she never spoke a word, she responded to us with hollering, or in non-verbal ways with the movement of her right arm and leg.

"Well, if she isn't feeling good, she probably doesn't feel much like smiling," I say.

"This is different," Carol insists. "I'm really worried about her." There is a pause as if Carol is going to say something else, but hesitates.

"I'm not sure if I should tell you this or not," she says.

After a long history together, now when Carol has something to tell me that she's not sure she should, I usually take a deep breath and tell her she can trust me and I will be okay knowing whatever it is.

"Well, that's up to you if you want to tell me," I say. "If you're afraid you're going to upset me, don't be. I'll be okay."

"Dad told me he dreamed that Annie died," Carol says.

Last year, shortly after she moved back in with Mom and Dad this time, Carol made a comment to me about how it is sometimes eerie living there. She said that once when she went into the family room, she found Annie dozing off in her wheelchair in front of the television. Annie was so still, Carol said, that she went over close to her to make sure she was still breathing. One morning Carol woke up late and didn't hear anything from downstairs. "I was afraid I might find all of them dead in their beds," she said. Although Carol and I both found a morbid humor in this and laughed at the absurdity of her comment at the time, this conversation set off a warning signal inside of me that had been dormant for years. I didn't think of Annie's death as being imminent. Why would she die? Of old age? She wasn't that old. And although she had far exceeded initial medical predictions of her life expectancy, I could see no reason she wouldn't continue on. So when Carol told me she thought about the real possibility of Annie's death because of her age, it threw me off for a minute. I suppose I had always been more worried about how we were going to manage taking care of Annie when Mom and Dad were gone.

Now, Carol tells me that Dad has dreamed about Annie's death. Some people might think that a dream is not a big deal, but it stirs and jostles me. In our family we believe in dreams, or at least that some people have special dreams. I'd never known my dad to have predictive dreams, but his mother, my grandmother, was a firm believer in hers. She never got the details of events completely correct, but she came close. Once she dreamed she was running from room to room in a hospital. She found out shortly afterwards that two of her daughters and her daughter-in-law were all expecting babies, who later were born within weeks of each other. Another time she dreamed that she was in a car accident. She didn't know how to drive, but usually rode to work with a younger woman, who in her view drove a little fast. Based on her dream, she changed her plans and got a ride with someone else that day. Nothing happened. She got to work and arrived home safely. But later that evening Grandma got a phone call with the news that her youngest son had been in a car accident. So when Carol tells me that Dad dreamed that Annie died, I take note.

"I'll come up tomorrow and see how she is," I offer.

I hang up the phone and immediately dial my sounding board, my husband Mark. I tell him about my conversation with Carol. I'm pretty shook up. I remember my dad's foreboding words on a vacation when Annie had gotten sick and was hospitalized. "Your sister Annie is not like most people," Dad said. "We can't expect her to live a long time." His words all those years ago come back as clearly as if he had spoken them yesterday.

I was little more than a year old when Annie was born in 1958, so my memories of childhood don't include a time before Annie. And my memories of Annie don't include a time when she wasn't disabled. I don't have a memory of learning that she wasn't going to be able to talk or walk or live as we did. She has always been here in my life with her disabilities fully present.

I never knew Annie in any other form than what she is, so although to the outside world she might not seem "normal," it is the only thing I know. In many ways, Annie's not being normal is in fact, normal to me. I never thought of Annie any other way, and I've never known life without her.

When I was still quite young I remember wishing, or maybe even praying, that I could share my life with my sister Annie. In the innocence of my child's worldview, I suggested to God that perhaps I could take Annie's place every other week. We could trade places and then she could have the chance to ride a bike, roller skate down the sidewalk, climb trees, have friends, go to parties and do all the things I loved to do.

Of course, a day came when I realized I was no longer willing to give up any of my life to trade places with her, and with this realization came a tremendous sense of guilt—not that any of it would have been possible anyway, and not that I was in any way responsible for Annie's condition. I realized that had I been born a year later, it would have been me in that wheelchair instead of her. Dwelling on that thought alone, it almost felt like, in some ways, it was me—only the me was her. It's convoluted thinking, I know, but having a sister with a profound disability had a profound effect on me.

"I don't know what I'll do if she dies," I tell Mark, and my voice starts shaking as I struggle to get out the rest of the words, "Annie is a big part of who I am. She is a part of me."

early 1960s

I let the screen door slam as I ran in the house calling out, "Aaaaanieee, where are you?" Annie was sitting with her legs elevated in the reclining chair Dad had made out of wood and Mom had padded with foam and covered with red corduroy. Two rounded, padded structures protruded from the back of her chair and supported both sides of her head, keeping it erect. "There you are Annie. Are you watching TV? Mommieee, can Annie come outside?"

Mom stepped into the living room with a basket of laundry in her arms and said, "No, Honey. I have work to do in here. Annie has to stay inside with me."

"Silly, Annie. Look what you did. You dropped your toy." I bent down and picked up the rattle. "Here you go, Annie." I held out the toy to her and waited patiently while Annie excitedly swung her right hand up and down two or three times before she grabbed onto it, then I turned and ran outside to play, the screen door slamming behind me.

1959 | I stand beside Annie shortly after her head was shaved for diagnostic testing.

CHAPTER 3 **A Mention of Feeding Tubes**

Day 2
Saturday July 25, 2009

I know that my parents are struggling. My mom is spending a lot of extra time taking care of Annie. My dad is having dementia issues and has become less helpful with Annie's care and more in need of assistance himself. When Carol called me yesterday to tell me about Dad's dream, she said Mom wants to take us up on our offer to help move her mother, my grandmother, from the assisted care facility she has been living at for several years, into a nursing home, on Monday. This move has been scheduled for several weeks, and I know this is bad news if Mom is waving a white flag and accepting this level of help with my grandmother. I had been offering help, and she had been refusing it for weeks running. Now all of a sudden she is willing to put Carol and me in charge of making sure all the personal items Grandma needs go with her and all the rest comes home. She is delegating to us the job of helping her mother settle into her new accommodations. This is not small.

Mom can't leave Annie because she feels like Annie is too sick.

I decide that when I go to my parents' house today I will prepare a couple of meals to leave with them so that Mom doesn't have to cook every night in the coming week.

Before my husband Mark, who is going to help me cook, and I leave our home in Cincinnati to drive the hour to where my parents live in Dayton, I cut up carrots, onions, celery and potatoes for a Crock-Pot stew that I plan to cook at Mom and Dad's house. I bring fresh green beans, a chicken, a bag of noodles, and the ingredients for apple crisp. I plan to make two meals that will provide dinner for the next four or five nights for them. I feel pretty good that this will be a welcome reprieve for my mother.

I can tell that things are not going well when we get to my parents' house the minute we arrive. No one meets us at the door. When I call out "Hello," my parents, who I usually find in the kitchen, answer that they are in Annie's room. Mark and I lug all the supplies into the kitchen. I pull out a large pot that he fills with water, and while he starts to cook the chicken, I go see Annie and my parents, walking through the dining room, across the corner of the living room, through the doorway, and down the long and dim hall to Annie's room.

Annie's room is painted a cheerful yellow and has sunlight streaming through the windows on two of the walls. Years ago Mom and Dad bought a hospital bed that is against the wall in the far corner of the room. Two Raggedy Ann dolls are suspended from the corner of the ceiling opposite Annie's bed so that she can more easily see them. A large dresser is against the wall under the dolls. It holds a cd player and stacks of cds of Annie's favorite music by Barry Manilow, Neil Diamond, Kenny Rogers and other country singers.

Annie's bed is kept in a raised position so that Mom and Dad can change her clothes and diapers without having to bend over. The amount of time they've spent doing that over the years is evident by the spot of threadbare carpet where they stand.

The head of the bed can also be elevated, and every afternoon my parents put Annie in bed in a reclined position, slightly lower than that of her wheelchair, in order to rest her back. Because they move her around during the day and let her sleep on her stomach at night, my parents have been remarkably successful at avoiding any bed sores over all these years of Annie's sedentary life. Unfortunately, however, after all these years in a wheelchair, Annie has a significant curvature of the spine.

A few weeks ago, I visited Mom and Dad to find my mom in a state of agitation. It was almost noon and Dad was over an hour late getting home from his regularly scheduled exercise at the hospital rehab center. Mom was waiting for him to get Annie up so she could feed her breakfast in the kitchen. I suggested and eventually convinced Mom to feed Annie in her bed. I am worried about both of my parents lifting Annie in and out of her bed at their ages, but I am adamant that my mom does not try to lift Annie by herself. I convinced Mom to put a TV in Annie's room so that Annie can stay in there all day if something happens and she needs to. Mom placed a chest of drawers at the foot of Annie's bed and got a cable installed for the television that they placed on top. We moved a small recliner into the room beside the bed so that someone could comfortably keep Annie company in there.

Today, when I enter the doorway to Annie's room, my dad is slouching in the recliner. My mom is sitting on a hard chair beside Annie, who is sitting in her custom-made reclined wheelchair in the middle of the room. Mom's face looks haggard, and she has not combed her hair. There is a sense of uncertainty or helplessness in the room.

I am shocked when I see Annie's face. Carol was not exaggerating. Annie looks worse than I expected. Her face is pale, almost gray, and her mouth is drooping on one side. She looks like a stroke victim. Her right arm is motionless at her side and looks completely foreign to me. I realize I have never seen it still like that before.

I walk over to her, lean over, and gently kiss her on the forehead. Instead of using my normal boisterous and cheerful tone of voice with her, I say, "Hi Sweetheart," in barely more than a whisper. "I'm sorry you're feeling bad, Sweetie."

I stand up and turn to my mom. "She looks like she feels terrible," I say. I know that Annie has been throwing up and hasn't had anything significant to eat or drink for days. What really worries my mom is that Annie hasn't had a wet diaper in over 24 hours. No one is voicing it out loud, but we are all hoping this is one of Annie's temporary fluctuations and not a sign of kidney failure. In the past when we'd gone on long trips in the car, or disrupted Annie's schedule in some way, she sometimes stopped wetting her diapers for a day, or even two. We are all waiting on edge for a wet diaper.

I am pretty sure Annie is dehydrated by now, and I start to wonder about the possibility of getting someone to give her an IV here at the house. "Maybe you shouldn't try to get her up out of bed," I suggest. "Maybe she would be more comfortable there."

"She's comfortable in her chair," Mom answers. "She likes her chair."

"That may be true, but she doesn't look comfortable right now," I argue. "When I get sick I like to be in my bed."

I can't believe the difference in Annie since I was last here a week ago. I knew that Annie had been sick with bronchitis and had visited the doctor in early June to get an antibiotic. By the end of June after she had finished the antibiotic, she got sores in her mouth from a Herpes virus and was grinding her teeth. The doctor prescribed a medicine for her over the phone. The mouth sores healed, and then last week Annie's fever returned. Mom and Dad took her back to the doctor who thought she had a sore throat and gave her a second round of antibiotics. Through the course of the last three or four weeks, Annie hadn't been feeling well and she hadn't been eating very much. Mom is struggling to do what the doctor ordered and get Annie to drink a glass of water every time she takes her antibiotic, four times a day. Annie doesn't drink water, or any other liquid actually, very well. Mom is not only worried and stressed out, she is exhausted.

The previous week when I had visited, Mom said that Annie was starting to feel better after her back-to-back bouts with bronchitis and the sores in her mouth. When I arrived there last week Annie was sitting in the kitchen in her chair, as she often did. She was happy and excited to see me. She smiled and hollered, and she started swinging her right arm up and down like usual. She was getting over the mouth sores and was feeling pretty good as far as I could tell.

But, never a good eater to begin with, through the course of the two illnesses Annie had refused to eat much of anything, and as a consequence she had lost some weight. Mom told me about this over the phone, but since Annie was always bone-thin anyway, I didn't notice a huge difference when I first saw her, until she bent her knee up and her loose pant-leg slipped to her thigh exposing her lower leg from the knee down.

"Wow," I said. Annie was now emaciated. Her knee looked huge on her tiny leg. Her bones were visible, with skin just draped over them. She looked like a Holocaust victim.

"I told you she lost weight," Mom said. "She couldn't eat with the sores in her mouth because she'd flinch every time we put the spoon in. But she's started eating better now."

"That's good," I said, "but how are you ever going to get her to eat enough to gain the weight back?"

I went over to Annie's chair to say goodbye before I left last week. I leaned over with my face close to hers, kissed her on the forehead, and said in a stern voice, "Annie, you've got to eat. You be a good girl. You need to eat."

This week Annie's condition has clearly deteriorated. At minimum, I feel certain she needs an IV for fluids. I tell Mom I think she should take Annie back to the doctor. From past experience Mom is skeptical about the doctors' abilities when it comes to diagnosing Annie, unless it is something like an ear infection that a doctor can actually see. She doesn't want Annie to have to be moved to the doctor's office where she might catch something even worse in her weakened state. Mom is especially hesitant to take Annie to a hospital where she will have to endure being poked with needles and IVs. She doesn't want Annie to have to go through that. She worries that the doctor may want to do something invasive that will send Annie into a seizure, further complicating the issue. Mom wants to stay on this course of treating Annie at home.

Before we leave to go home, Mom brings up the subject of a feeding tube for the first time. Since May, Annie has had a caregiver, Christiana, come to the house once or twice a week. Mom has trained Christiana to feed Annie. "Christiana says she has several clients with feeding tubes and they do really well with them," Mom says. I feel like someone has just twisted my insides like a wet towel. Internally I balk, thinking, No. Don't put Annie on a feeding tube. When you put someone on a feeding tube frequently someone else has to make the decision to take her back off the feeding tube later. I do not want to be that someone.

I don't say anything.

mid 1960s

Carol and I, two little blond-haired girls in matching homemade red and blue shorts and little sleeveless shirts, played in the far end of the yard near the gravel alley. I was swinging high, but not too high, on the metal swing set. Carol jumped off her swing in mid-air and ran over to the old cherry tree.

"Teene! Come here quick!"

I dragged my feet on the brown dusty dirt patch where the grass had worn away beneath the swing. When the swing slowed to a gentle sway, I jumped off and ran over to where Carol was squatting underneath the cherry tree.

"It's a baby bird!" Carol was pointing to a small gray down-covered bird huddled against the trunk of the tree. I looked up into the limbs of the gnarled tree that we loved to climb and saw a small nest perched near the top.

"It fell out of that nest."

"Let's tell Mom!" she said, and Carol was off and running towards the house with me close on her heels. Carol ran across the cement patio on the side of the house, jerked open the screen door, and charged up the three steps to the kitchen yelling, "Mom!" She came to an abrupt halt on the linoleum floor of the kitchen, and I slammed into her, causing her to lose her balance and stumble forwards another step. Uh-oh. Mom's feeding Annie.

Mom was sitting at the kitchen table, with Annie facing her in her reclined wheelchair pulled up alongside on the right. An open jar of baby food and a sipper cup were on the table. Mom held an empty spoon in her right hand poised above Annie's head. Annie was laughing and coughing. With her left hand, Mom was trying to cover Annie's mouth with a corner of the terry cloth towel that was draped like a bib around her neck. Mom was covered with tiny speckles of baby food that Annie sprayed all over when she heard us come in and started to laugh. Sticky speckles were on Mom's face and all over her clothes. They stuck in her stiff-sprayed-60s-style hair-do like some sort of bizarre banana-scented light brown confetti. She looked at us girls with exasperation. "I told you girls not to come running in here when I am trying to feed Annie," she said.

We were standing in single file, with our heads bowed. "We're sorry," we said in identical unison voices.

"Well, what did you come in here hollering about?" Mom quietly asked.

Very calmly and quietly Carol said, "I found a baby bird."

"Where?"

"Under the cherry tree."

"Well, don't touch it. It might be sick. And its mother might not come back to help it if you touch it."

"Okay." Again the identical voices in unison.

Carol turned around, grabbed my arm, and pulled me quietly from the room the way we had come. We tiptoed down the stairs, slowly, ever so carefully, and without the tiniest of sound, we opened the screen door, slid out onto the patio, and softly, ever so quietly, closed the door behind us.

1962 | Carol and Me

CHAPTER 4 **Mom's Optimism**

Day 3
Sunday July 26

Mom is encouraged and optimistic when I call her first thing in the morning. Annie soaked her Attends and all her bedding overnight. Mom is relieved—at least Annie's kidneys are working. This averts a 911 call and trip to the hospital this morning.

Mom believes the antibiotic is upsetting Annie's stomach and is responsible for the whole problem of Annie throwing up and not eating.

"I'm not giving her anymore of the antibiotic," she says. "I'm just going to keep giving her clear liquids."

"I agree that she needs liquids," I say. "I think she is dehydrated. You feel and look really bad when you are dehydrated." I remember this from my last pregnancy when I got the flu and landed in the hospital for 24 hours to get re-hydrated.

Mom also tells me she is going to make some phone calls about the possibility of getting an IV for Annie at home. I think this is the best plan if we can figure it out.

That would avoid the dreaded trip to a hospital where Mom loses control of taking care of Annie, but where no one else knows how. It's just really hard with Annie, because no one, including her doctor, wants to put her through a lot of invasive tests. And a major upset can send her right into a seizure, which is never good.

"I'm not going to do anything today," Mom says, "until I talk to the doctor tomorrow."

But Mom is hopeful for the first time that Annie might be able to come out of this. I can hear it in her voice, and I recognize her indomitable spirit rising. She has explained it all away with the antibiotic.

My mom's optimism is legendary. This is a natural mode of behavior for her. It's not that I don't believe things could be turning around for Annie; it's just that I've seen my mom's optimism in action before. Her optimism borders on denial at times. I'm also plagued by the memory that Annie first threw up a couple of months ago on the very first day that Christiana came to help back in May, and then on another occasion about a month later. It is very rare for Annie to be sick to her stomach. She hates to throw up, and she really struggles not to if she's sick. So the fact that she has thrown up twice in the recent past nags the back of my mind.

"You might be right about the antibiotic," I say, "but Annie started throwing up back in May before she ever started on this medicine."

"She could have done that because she was stressed," Mom explains. "She could probably sense that I was anxious about Christiana coming to take care of her."

I let it go because Annie does pick up on my mom's emotions, and it is true that Mom was stressed out about turning Annie's care over to someone else.

I allow Mom the benefit of the doubt on this, but I also don't believe that either a bacterial infection or the antibiotic is causing all this trouble with Annie's not eating and her throwing up. I fear that Annie may have a serious problem with her digestive system. Because of her curvature of the spine, who knows what Annie's internal organs look like?

Mom mentions the idea of a feeding tube again. I remain uncertain about it. I know how difficult it has been for Mom to feed Annie and get her to eat her whole life. I know what a worry and stress it is. Even though I am opposed to this kind of intervention for Annie, I decide to support Mom with whatever decision she makes about it. We have to trust Mom's lead on all of this. She really does know best when it comes to Annie.

If Annie recovers from her current condition and needs help regaining her strength, maybe a feeding tube makes sense for everybody, especially my mom. I'm looking ahead at the situation my mom is getting into trying to take care of Annie while my dad declines with Alzheimer's. A feeding tube would take a lot of stress and actual physical effort out of my mom's life. I'm not going to oppose her on this.

For the time being I succumb to Mom's optimism. I hope maybe the impending crisis has passed.

Before we hang up Mom relays an anecdote. She tells me that this morning she heard Carol calling from Annie's room, for her to "Come quickly." Mom hurried into the room where Carol was dancing to a song by Neil Diamond, and Annie was smiling for the first time in several days. Mom is nearly elated as she tells me this story. She says, "I was afraid I would never see her smile again."

1958–1964

When Diane Louise, later to be nicknamed Annie, was born, she seemed like a perfectly normal infant. She opened her eyes and looked at my parents; she smiled. I think she even cried, although my mom says that she rarely cried under normal circumstances. The days following her painful diagnostic testing were the exception. Things had to be pretty bad for her to cry, and I can't remember ever seeing her do it.

When Annie was born, my parents thought they had another healthy daughter.

My parents first began to suspect something was wrong when Annie was about nine months old and wouldn't sit up by herself. My dad took her to the doctor's office for her regular check-up and when he laid her on the examining table, our family physician Dr. Thompson asked, "She's not sitting up yet?" Dad held Annie under her arms and sat her up, but she just kind of wobbled around. "I want to get you an appointment at Children's Hospital in Columbus," Dr. Thompson said.

Dr. Thompson wasn't overly concerned, however; he thought there might be something wrong with Annie's back.

Annie was fourteen months old, not sitting up, crawling, or walking when my parents took her to Columbus, but they still weren't overly concerned. My mom's biggest fear was that Annie might not be able to go to school. She thought that would be a terrible thing.

One of the first doctors who looked at Annie in Columbus said, "There can't be much wrong with her; look at her face. Her eyes are bright and she is smiling at me."

The doctor initially thought it was a hematoma, a collection of blood outside of a blood vessel that occurs because the wall of a blood vessel, artery, vein or capillary, has been damaged. The doctor told my parents that surgeons would likely just go into her head through the soft spot, repair the hematoma, and she would probably be all right. For confirmation he wanted her to see a neurologist, Dr. Shorer.

This was in 1959, before MRIs and CT scans. Dr. Shorer did what my mom remembers being called an "air test." They shaved off all of Annie's hair and stuck needles into her head all over. Mom remembers that the doctor said Annie was lucky because she still had a soft spot on her head, so that they wouldn't have to drill. They put dye in Annie's spinal column, and then they put air in and extracted it out through the needles somehow. The dye was supposed to be in certain specific places in her brain.

I later found out from Annie's medical records that the test was called a pneumoencephalogram or PEG. In a PEG the cerebrospinal fluid is drained to a small amount from around the brain and replaced with air, oxygen or helium to allow the structure of the brain to show up more clearly on an x-ray picture.

Medical researchers would later acknowledge that pneumoencephalography was extremely painful, very dangerous, and not well tolerated by patients.

The test made Annie extremely ill. She was so sick she wouldn't move and she couldn't keep any food down. She screamed when Mom would wake her up to feed her, even though Mom was being extremely careful not to jostle her. But Mom persisted because she had to get Annie to drink and keep down a certain amount of liquid over a 24-hour period before they'd let her go home. Mom was giving Annie two ounces of formula at a time, and every time she fed her, she fed her twice. The first time, Annie vomited it back up, but the second bottle she kept down.

My father has always believed the test caused permanent stroke-like damage that resulted in Annie's left arm becoming nearly unusable and her left leg becoming stiff and difficult to move. Following the testing, Annie started having seizures for which she took Phenobarbital and Dilantin her entire life.

My dad was back home with the Carol and me, and my mom was alone with Annie, when the doctors came into Annie's hospital room and told Mom the results of the test.

The PEG results showed channels and blockages in Annie's brain that were not normal. The problem was determined to be prenatal in origin and was diagnosed as a congenital cerebral defect of undetermined type. My parents now believe that Annie's brain damage may have been caused when my mom had a high fever from the Asian flu while she was pregnant with her.

The test results were a shock. Annie had severe brain damage. Neither my mom, nor my dad, ever expected the news to be that bad. And according to

Mom, neither did any of the doctors. "You have never seen doctors so surprised in your life," she told me.

She said she asked them a lot of questions, but they "evaded" answering them. Mom was given the basic impression that Annie wasn't going to progress as fast as most people and that her motor skills wouldn't be as good.

"When I first heard, I thought she would be disabled," Mom said, "but I didn't have any idea how disabled." Annie was still a baby at the time, so the fact that she couldn't yet speak or walk didn't mean that she never would speak or walk. My parents didn't know what Annie might eventually be able to do.

They went back to Columbus several times on follow-up visits. Mom said, "Every time we'd go back they'd tell us a little more. Each time they added a little more to the problem."

The doctors told my parents that if you drew a line from in front of one ear across the top of Annie's head to the other ear, the portion of her brain in front of the line was gone. They said that, as best they could tell, she had the equivalent of a lobotomy.

"I had one awakening moment," Mom said, "when I was talking to Dr. Thompson and he said, 'You have two choices: you can keep her and take care of her, or put her in an institution.' I had one moment of thinking that I didn't know what I was going to be dealing with."

My parents were unwilling to put their tiny baby in an institution. And although with this revelation of Annie's condition the future became a real big scary thing, my mom felt she really didn't have a choice. She and my dad weren't willing to give Annie up any more than they were willing to give up me or Carol.

At one point the doctors told my parents that Annie probably wouldn't live longer than eight years. They told Mom and Dad to take her home and love her. So they did.

At first Annie really wasn't any more trouble than any other baby, once they got her seizures under control with medication. She just never grew out of the needs of a baby.

As an adult with children of my own, I can't even imagine how devastating Annie's diagnosis must have been for my parents. But the truth is, I don't really know how either of my parents felt about Annie's diagnosis and prognosis. They never spoke of it. "I had other children," Mom said, "I had a lot to do that kept my mind occupied."

I never heard my parents speak one word about wishing things were different, or wishing Annie wasn't disabled. I think once they reassured themselves that there was nothing that could be done; they just accepted how she was and went on. I think perhaps expressing any disappointment, devastation, or wish that things were different in some ways would have seemed a bit like denying Annie's value as she was. They loved her. It was that simple. And she seemed happy—always.

Mostly, by bringing Annie home and integrating her into our family life, my parents allowed me to love her as well. It was easy to do.

1958 | Annie's disabilities were not evident at this early age.

CHAPTER 5

A Call to Dr. Ryan

Day 4

Monday July 27

On Grandma's moving day I arrive in Dayton early in the morning. I have an overnight bag packed in my trunk in case the day goes long and I am too tired to drive home to Cincinnati later. I go in to see Annie briefly and can't discern any noticeable improvement from when I saw her on Saturday.

Since my grandfather died in 1993, my mom has been devoted to taking care of her mother. When Grandma's dementia became a problem, Mom, Dad and Annie traveled to Piqua one day a week to help my grandma so that she could remain in her home as long as possible. Over the past five years or so, my mom has been preoccupied and stressed out by Grandma's deteriorating condition.

I felt that Mom had her hands full already taking care of Annie. Then, when my dad's Alzheimer's symptoms started, I tried to encourage Mom to step back from her mother's care and delegate more to her sister and brother. "They don't have a spouse with Alzheimer's and a disabled adult child they are taking care of," I said, to no avail.

The fact that Mom does not go with Carol and me today to move Grandma speaks volumes. I offered to stay home with Annie if she wanted to go with Carol but Mom is unwilling to leave the house while Annie is this sick.

Carol and I spend the entire day in Piqua moving Grandma's personal items and clearing out her old room. It's about 5:00 p.m. by the time we leave Grandma settled in at her new nursing home. This project has taken much longer than we ever anticipated and was much more stressful. I'm beat and glad I packed my overnight bag; I only need to make it back to Dayton. I'm also feeling rather proud and happy that Carol and I protected our mom from having to do this chore.

Annie doesn't seem any better when we get back. After Mom and Dad put her to bed for the night, they join me in the family room. I give them a shortened version of Grandma's move, then the conversation shifts to Annie.

Mom is happy that Annie ate a small amount of yogurt today. My parents are still discussing the merits of a feeding tube. The worry about how to help Annie regain her strength weighs heavy on their minds. I am concerned that her condition is not improving.

A couple of tablespoons of yogurt a day is not going to be enough to undo the damage that the days, weeks really, of not eating have wrought on Annie's little body. I look them both in the eyes and speak slowly for emphasis. "I don't believe Annie is going to get better on her own," I tell them. "She's getting worse. I think she needs to see the doctor again."

"He just saw her last Wednesday," Mom says.

"She looked a lot different last Wednesday," I counter. "The doctor has not seen how she looks now." I pause, not wanting to make things worse for my parents, but also not wanting to remain silent if there is something that can, and should, be done for Annie. "I think she's in trouble," I say.

"I just don't want to have to take her out when she is weak like this," Mom says.

I feel like we've been in a fog of confusion about what to do for Annie. We sit in the family room weighing our options. Although my dad is slipping away more and more every day as Alzheimer's wrecks havoc on his brain, he has a moment of clarity and says, "We can call Tim Ryan." Tim Ryan is a friend of the family and a retired physician. "Tim has told me on more than one occasion to call him if we ever need anything," Dad says. "Maybe he will come over and look at Diane tomorrow." Dad always calls Annie by her given name, Diane. When I was small and unable to pronounce "Diane" I shortened her name to Annie and it stuck, for everybody that is, except my dad.

I spend the night on an air mattress on the family room floor of my parents' house. Sometime in the night, I wake up and turn on the second intercom connected to Annie's room that my parents keep there. I listen to the steady rhythm of Annie's breathing. I listen in case something's wrong and Mom needs my help. In case something's wrong and Mom doesn't hear. In case.

1960s–1970s

In 1964 when Annie was six-years old, my parents took her back to a local hospital to see if there was anything else they could do for her. They wanted to know if she could benefit from speech therapy or some other treatment. Annie saw a team of doctors at this time. The doctors wanted to do an EEG, which records electro activity along the scalp through a series of electrodes placed on the scalp. After my parents' experience with the PEG in Columbus, they refused the test. The doctors examined Annie and reviewed her previous test results. A conference was held on her behalf.

The physical findings read as follows:

"The PEG report and the previous findings of this child reveal evidence of considerable loss of cerebral substance. Psychologically, the child appears to be functioning at about a three or four month level, and we believe that this state of development has been rather stationary for some period of time."

The neurologist wrote in his report, "I do not feel that there is any further workup that needs to be done on this child, and the only service to this family is to reassure them that they are doing all that can be done."

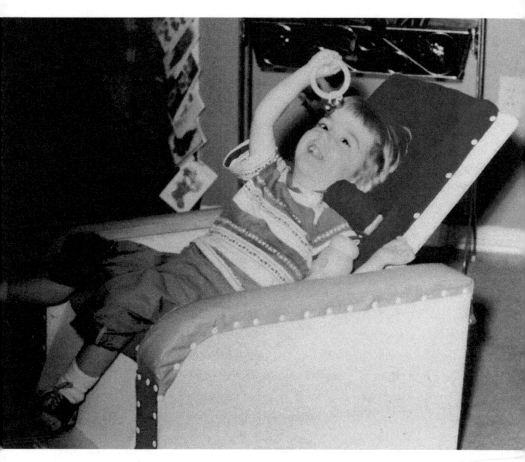

circa 1961 | *Annie reclines in a chair Dad made.*

CHAPTER 6

Dancing to Neil Diamond

Day 5
Tuesday July 28

Carol springs into Annie's room, turns on the stereo and says, "We're going to play Neil Diamond. Should it be 'Sweet Caroline' or 'Brother Love's Traveling Salvation Show?'" She doesn't wait for a response. "'Brother Love,'" she says. She turns the track on, turns up the volume, and starts to dance around the room.

Annie turns her head to look at Carol from her hospital bed in the corner of the room where she reclines in an elevated position. Her nearly transparent skin provides a thin cover for her bones. Her face is pale and drawn, highlighting her dark, nearly black eyes in contrast. As Carol spins around the room, Mom and I stand beside Annie's bed and search her eyes for, and then recognize, a glimmer of light. Annie's lips twitch and Mom says, "She's trying to smile."

Carol starts singing along with Neil Diamond as she dances. "What is your silly sister doing, Annie?" I ask. Mom and I laugh, and Annie's mouth opens slightly and turns up at the corners. It is not the vibrant, radiant smile that we are accustomed to and that she wears in the photograph on her dresser, but it is a smile nevertheless. We all feel rewarded.

The smile fades, as does the song and the dance. Annie closes her eyes. She is tired. The party has zapped her strength. Carol walks over close to Annie and repeats a mantra she's started saying to her. "No worries," Carol says.

Mom leans over and places her hands on the sides of Annie's face. She kisses her forehead and says, "Maybe you'll smile again later."

A little later in the morning, Dr. Ryan shows up at the house carrying his black medical bag. He is tall and slim with gray thinning hair. His kind eyes are blue as they look through the wire-rim glasses he wears. He walks slowly with his shoulders hunched and a bit of a limp. I feel like I am in a TV show from the early sixties when the doctor comes to call.

Dr. Ryan is very gentle as he checks Annie over. He's known our family for over twenty-five years and he realizes my parents are skeptical about the ability of medical professionals to help Annie. He knows that my parents want to avoid a trip to the ER at all costs.

Dr. Ryan thinks he hears a slight rattle in Annie's chest—the remnants of last month's bronchitis. "She needs to stay on the antibiotic," he says. "And she looks like she could use a little help with the fluids."

"I've learned some things over the past few days that I think are going to help me get her to eat and drink better," Mom says, referring to her new method of squeezing liquid one drop at a time from a baby bottle through an enlarged hole in the nipple.

We leave Annie and walk out to the living room with Dr. Ryan. He reminisces about a medical case or two he's seen in the past. "You know the time comes when we all have to die," Dr. Ryan says. "It's because of the exceptional care you've given her that she's lived all these fifty-some years. You're doing everything that you can for her."

After Dr. Ryan leaves, Mom becomes determined to get fluids down Annie. She has placed a timer on the kitchen counter and is setting it to go off at 30-minute intervals, when she will try to get Annie to drink another ounce or two from the bottle of sweet tea she squeezes into her mouth a few drops at a time.

Mom takes Annie's temperature and it's still 100 degrees. Annie throws up some of the small amount of liquid she drank a few minutes earlier.

Dad and I sit at the kitchen table, not able to find any way to be helpful. "When I took her to Columbus Children's Hospital shortly after she was born," Dad says, "your mother fed her every ten minutes so that she would eat what the doctors required for her release." Mom wasn't seventy-five-years old when they took Annie to Columbus, I think.

The 30-minute timer goes off, and Mom tries to get Annie to drink a few more ounces of water. I follow her into Annie's room where she stands at the side of Annie's bed and leans her arm on the metal bar of the safety rail. It looks un-comfortable to me. "Do you want me to wrap a towel or something around the railing to pad it for you?" I ask.

Mom tells me to get a piece of foam padding that she keeps in Annie's closet and a ribbon from a drawer in her bedroom to tie it on with. I find a 2-inch wide, gross-grain, lime green ribbon in my mom's room that I cut into three 12-inch long pieces. I cut the foam pad into a size that will wrap nicely around the metal railing and tie it in place with the three ribbons.

The day progresses like a bad one-act play.

Annie throws up.

Mom buries her head in her hands at the kitchen table and says, "I am tired of trying to make decisions about what to do when I don't know what to do."

"We keep pushing liquids, like the doctor said," Dad responds.

The 30-minute timer goes off and Mom fills another bottle with sugar water.

I wonder how long my mother can keep up this pace.

Carol tells me she tries to communicate with Annie's soul and spirit. "Annie's soul is tired," she says.

Dad tells me when he puts Annie to bed every night he has a hard time leaving the room—leaving her alone. He tells me he had a dream that he hopes he never has to live to see— the day when he has to see Annie in a coffin.

"I hope I never have to see the day after both you and Mom are gone and Annie is looking for you, not understanding, and waiting for you to return," I say.

Carol tells Dad that he can communicate with Annie's other dimensions besides her physical self —he can talk to her spirit and soul. "Her spirit and soul are not suffering like her physical body is right now," she says.

I don't know if Dad believes what Carol is telling him, or if he even understands anymore what a spirit and soul are. But Carol's words give me comfort in what I feel is becoming a hopeless and helpless situation. We are not able to connect with Annie through words. She can't speak and we have no way to know if she understands the words we say. We think she at least understands the mood or essence of what we say. So in some ways, I suppose we always have communicated with Annie on some kind of soul or spiritual level. Although I try at times to do what Carol suggests, Annie's emaciated and pain-wracked physical body functions as a barrier between me and another existence or place where her soul and spirit are not suffering. Still, Carol's adamant belief in these other pain-free realms of existence for Annie gives me hope.

Mom walks over and looks at the chart she's made of Annie's medicines: Dilantin and Phenobarbital for seizures, Tylenol for fever, Phenergan for nausea, Keflex for whatever might be causing her fever. "It's time for her antibiotic again," Mom says.

Mom sets the timer for another 30 minutes.

Dad prays Novenas and Hail Marys.

I chase visions of an empty wheelchair from my mind.

Carol sees Annie in a golden light—dancing to Neil Diamond.

1960s–1970s

When Annie was still pretty young, some well-meaning doctor provided braces to help her sit up. We have a picture of Annie sitting on the sofa wearing braces on her neck, on her torso, on each leg. She looks like she is in one big body brace. No one likes to look at that photo. People gasp when they see that picture. It's an "Oh my God, look at that poor child!" kind of picture. The braces were one of the first of a series of experiments my parents tried with Annie in an effort to improve her situation.

One time we tried physical therapy with her. Dad placed Annie on her stomach on the kitchen table that was padded with blankets or towels. Then he put one of his hands on either side of her head. The rest of us stood around the table with a specific designated job. Mom took one side of Annie's body while Carol and I held Annie's arm or leg on the other. We moved her limbs in a synchronized fashion with my dad turning her head. Dad said, "Left" and gently lifted and turned Annie's head to her right side. At the same time Mom stretched Annie's left arm and leg out and up in a turtle-like motion. Then we switched. Dad said, "Right" and moved her head to the left, while the left arm and leg came back down. On the other side of the table, Carol and I bent the right arm and leg up. We did this for several minutes. I was pretty young at the time, so I didn't exactly know the theory behind what we were doing, or if it even worked in any measurable way. I just did what I was told, "Right—up, left—down."

In the sixties and early seventies there wasn't a lot of help for people with disabilities. If you wanted something done, you had to do it yourself. Annie needed to recline because she couldn't hold her head up very well, and they didn't make a chair that would work for her. So Dad built them. They always had an elevated footrest and a reclined back with a pillow for her neck.

From an early age we learned how to help Annie when her head fell out of her pillow, or when she slid down in her chair. "Christine, could you fix

Annie?" my mom would say while she was busy with a household chore. I'd stand behind Annie's chair, take her head in my hands, and gently place it back in her neck pillow, adjusting the pillow with the hope that it might stay in place a little longer this time. Then I'd slide my hands behind her back and under her arms and tug her back up into place in her chair. "Fixing Annie" was second nature to us.

You might say that Annie was lucky because my dad was a tool and die maker by trade, and a motivated, creative designer and builder by nature. He was able, and willing, to teach himself what he needed, or wanted, to know how to do. Dad built all of Annie's chairs for her until she was in her twenties. I can remember at least four: two wooden ones that were used in the house; one made of a metal frame that looked sort of like a reclined high chair on wheels—we used that one like a stroller; and later when Annie outgrew the metal one, Dad made one of fiberglass. I remember standing in the garage and watching him as he took strips of a fabric substrate and dipped them through a bucket of viscous liquid, then smoothed them onto the frame and structure that was becoming Annie's chair. It reminded me of our paper mache craft projects in grade school. Dad built a frame with wheels that he could attach to the chair to convert it to a stroller. They also used the chair as a car seat. Mom is pushing Annie in the fiberglass chair with wheels in a picture from a trip we took to Myrtle Beach. And the fiberglass chair, without the wheels, is sitting on the sand under an umbrella on the beach in another photo. So it was a pretty versatile chair.

One time when I was in high school, a physical therapist came to the house and brought a walker for Annie, like the little walkers with wheels for babies that have now been banned. This walker was bigger, and quite frankly looked a little scary and spider-like to me with its long metal bars. Annie sat upright in a canvas sling-type seat in the middle of it. My dad put her in it one night while my mom was gone, and he must have left her in it too long because I think she nearly passed out, and then she threw up. My mom was more than upset about what happened. She was the chief commander and head caretaker when it came to Annie. They got rid of the walker.

Annie had glasses once. My parents figured out that her vision wasn't as good as it should be, probably about the time Carol and I were both getting glasses. They took her to a specialist who was able to use a special instrument to determine the prescription she needed. Annie got glasses; they were that dark brown plastic frame type so popular in the seventies. But she wouldn't leave them on her face, just like she wouldn't leave mine on my face if I got too close to her and wasn't paying attention. Although Annie wasn't able to productively use her left arm, she compensated with her right. She had good control, quickness, and a lot of strength in her right hand and arm, and she liked to grab things. We learned that the hard way with our hair, until we figured out it was always best to hold Annie's right hand when we got close to her. If you weren't paying attention, she could get a hold of your hair and tangle it around her fingers before you knew what happened. Sometimes she'd get your hair so tangled up you needed to call someone to help you extricate yourself from her strong grasp.

Annie's glasses didn't last very long. I only remember them because she is wearing them in one of our annual Easter photos, where Dad is holding her upright in his arms with Mom standing beside them on our front porch.

Probably the most promising and disappointing experiment was the school. Mom sent Annie to a school for the handicapped when I was in high school. Annie was probably about fifteen-years old at the time. Mom had a lot of trepidation about doing this, but decided with encouragement to give it a try. It would free up six or seven hours a day. Mom could go to the store, go visit a friend, walk over to the neighbors, walk around the block, sit outside and stare at the clouds—she would have all kinds of freedom. I can still see my mom standing beside the bus with her shoulders hunched up and her arms crossed defensively in front of her chest, as Annie's wheelchair slowly ascended on the electric lift and disappeared into the bus. The school worked out okay at first, and Annie seemed to like it. But then the school system moved her school to the other side of town, and Annie had a very long bus ride. They wouldn't let her recline on the bus; she had to sit up straight. The first day of school when she returned home, she was leaning way out over the arm of her chair, with her head hanging down. Mom was livid. That was Annie's last day of school.

circa 1972 | Mom watches Annie get on the bus to go to school.

CHAPTER 7 **A Call for Help**

Day 6
Wednesday July 29

When I call from home today, Mom is willing to talk to me for a few minutes. She tells me Annie's fever is almost gone, and she has been able to consume small amounts of Ensure. She says Annie looks better, but that she has a long road to go to build her strength back up and regain the weight she lost.

December 2008–May 2009

When I was young, I worried a lot about Annie dying, but as we both grew older I started worrying less about her dying and more about what would happen to her if Mom and Dad died. I worried more about what would be asked of me regarding Annie's care, or what I would expect of myself, and how I would handle it now that I had four children of my own.

Would I have to take care of Annie? Would I be able to? Would taking care of her mean I wouldn't be free to travel to visit my out-of-town children?

Sometimes I thought maybe Annie would be the first to die. And then I thought about how that would break my parents' hearts. So I tried to determine which ending scenario would be the best. I thought, maybe if Dad died first Mom would survive better than he would taking care of Annie alone. And then I thought, after that, maybe it would be a relief for Mom if Annie died second, so that Mom wouldn't have to worry about Annie missing her, or who would take care of her. But then Mom would be alone and wouldn't have my Dad to help her with the heartbreak. I couldn't think of a good solution. So I gave up trying. I remembered that I was not God, and it wasn't my problem to solve, even if I wanted to. Instead of trying to think of the best solution when it came time for my parents and Annie to leave this life, I prayed to God, "In your infinite wisdom, only you know what will be best. Please be kind and merciful."

When my friends asked, "What are you going to do about Annie when your parents die?" I told them, "I don't think about it anymore."

"I feel bad knowing you are going to be left dealing with this," my mom once told me.

"The best thing you can do for us is to get someone else trained to care for her," I responded. This was probably during one of several conversations I had with Mom encouraging her to seek out more support for Annie's care. And several years ago Mom did sign Annie up with the Montgomery County Developmental Disabilities Services (DDS). She found out about the services they offered and even got their newsletter, but she refused to act on any of it to get help with taking care of Annie. By this point, I guess she was used to taking care of her, and she wasn't willing to relinquish that to someone else.

Meanwhile, I sat with Mom and generated detailed lists of Annie's medicine, her meals, her daily schedule, and how to generally care for her. I kept a copy, and Mom put a copy in an envelope on the wall of Annie's room. Mom and

Dad had aged into their seventies and Annie and I were in our late forties. I worried that something might happen to my Mom, and I had visions of being in the house, trying to take care of Annie, and not knowing how much medicine to give her, or how often, or what to do if she got into a bad cough-ing fit while Mom was unconscious in a hospital bed somewhere. I really did not want to find myself in that vulnerable situation.

For the time being, everything seemed to be on a steady keel, even though I felt in some ways we were sitting on a powder keg ready to explode with little to no notice as my parents aged into their mid-seventies.

It was in 2007 or 2008, that my mom started noticing problems with my dad's memory, in particular with his sense of time. He seemed to never know the day of the week, and he was waking up every morning thinking it was Sunday and trying to get ready for church. By November of 2008, Mom went with Dad for a doctor's appointment, during which he was evaluated and diagnosed with early-stage Alzheimer's.

Mostly Dad was doing okay, although he was lethargic and less emotionally involved in his surroundings. He was still driving at the time, but had started having trouble finding his car in the parking garage at the hospital, where he went regularly to exercise. One day he forgot to feed Annie when he was watching her while my Mom was out for lunch. Mom came home and found Annie's food in the microwave when she was making herself a cup of tea. The medicine Mom had measured out for Annie and left on the counter top was gone. So Dad must have put the food in the microwave, given Annie her medicine, and then cleaned her up, skipping over the part about feed-ing her. This new development in Dad's condition was unsettling for all of us, but especially for my mom who felt she no longer could trust him with Annie's care.

Dad's condition came to a crisis point in December of 2008. My dad's young-est brother, my Uncle Mike, had a massive heart attack. Just a few days later, my dad's brother Tom's wife, my Aunt Nancy, suffered a massive stroke. My aunt and uncle were both hospitalized in Piqua where they lived, and where my dad grew up. My parents wanted to be there as much as they could to support their family members.

Carol was living out of town at the time. I went to Dayton as much as I could to stay with Annie during the day so my parents could visit the hospital.

When my Uncle Mike died about a week after he had his heart attack, we managed the logistics of getting my parents to the visitation and the funeral. My Aunt Nancy, who was found to be without significant brain function, was expected to die within days.

I was babysitting Annie on a Tuesday while my parents were at a routine doctor's appointment when my Aunt MaryLou called to tell us my Aunt Nancy had died shortly after noon. I was upset, and I called my husband Mark, and then I called Jim.

Jim was my boyfriend for two years in high school, and he now worked for Montgomery County DDS. Without fail, every five years at our high school reunions Jim asked about Annie and my parents. Over the phone that first day, I explained what was going on in my family. I told him about my dad's dementia.

"My parents need some help. For all these years they've taken care of Annie by themselves and have never asked for any help," I said with a shaking voice and tears flowing down my face, as I looked out the window and away from Annie where she sat quietly listening in her chair.

I went into Annie's closet and pulled out the metal box that contained all of her important papers, then sat down on the sofa while Jim and I tried to sort out over the phone what Annie's status was with DDS and what kind of assistance she qualified for. Jim assured me they could provide some kind of help and said he would do some searching around on his own for records about Annie. I promised to call him back in January after things settled down from the two funerals and the holidays. When I told my parents about my phone conversation with Jim, they seemed reassured by the prospect or possibility of getting some regular help with Annie.

My Dad had a significant incident over the weekend of my aunt's funeral that precipitated a second visit to the doctor. My dad's sister and her husband drove Mom and Dad to the funeral. Dad remembered riding up to Piqua, but then didn't know how he got "access" to the house he was in once they arrived back home in Dayton. When asked, he thought he was home, but he also thought he was still in Piqua. For a while, every day following the funeral trip, usually after dinner while sitting at the kitchen table in the home they had lived in for nearly 30 years, Dad said, "I just can't figure out how I got to be here…" My mom tried walking with him to the corner so he could read the street sign and see that it was the street they had lived on for all these years in Dayton. But somehow in Dad's mind there was a disconnect.

My mom was worried he might wander off trying to get back "home." She took him back to the doctor who gave him a prescription for Aricept. The doctor thought the stress of the situation with two family deaths in such a short period of time could have caused the new problem Dad was having and that it might be temporary.

Meanwhile, my concern about Dad ratcheted up. And my concern for how Mom was going to take care of Annie skyrocketed.

I determined to stay the course with DDS and see that my parents took a step, however small, in getting some help with Annie. Over the next months and after several meetings with various DDS personnel, Annie's situation was assessed and we learned that she qualified for a significant amount of money to pay for at-home health care providers. With this DDS support, my parents could pay for someone to take care of Annie every day if they wanted to. This was a tremendous relief for me to learn. My parents remained reluctant. They had an elderly woman named Vera they could call occasionally to take care of Annie, and they felt like they were managing okay on their own. They had fears that the unknown caregiver might mistreat Annie, and they didn't like the idea of having strangers coming into their home and invading their privacy to care for Annie when they were perfectly capable of doing it themselves.

Annie was assigned a DDS caseworker, Rob, who was probably in his late thirties or early forties. He was soft-spoken and carried a sense of optimism with his presence. Although Annie could have gotten help every day of the week, with Rob and me both advocating more help, and Mom reluctant to have any, we compromised at having a home health aide come once or twice a week to help with Annie's baths and changing the bed linens.

During the process of identifying a service and caregiver, I accompanied my parents and Annie to every meeting and interview because at this point, my dad's mental faculties were continuing to erode. He sat through the meetings largely as an observer, sometimes listening to his iPod through his earphones and only occasionally making a comment or asking a question. I didn't want my mom to feel alone through the process, so I tagged along with my own questions and opinions.

We went to a DDS fair where we were able to talk to many home health care providers. We generated a list of companies we would like to consider and then set up interviews. Finally we settled on a company, and they sent us Christiana for an interview. When I answered the doorbell, a tall and thin attractive young woman with long black hair and deep brown eyes stood there. She was wearing large hoop earrings. I noticed because I was worried about a confrontation between the earrings and Annie's notorious right hand.

We sat down in the living room, and at first Christiana was quiet and seemed timid, but as the interview progressed, she started looking over at Annie who was sitting close by. Christiana started smiling at Annie, and Annie responded in her usual fashion with a quick and exuberant smile of her own.

I felt for the first time in my life that everything might be okay.

1984 | Annie reaches for a Raggedy Ann doll I made for her at Christmas.

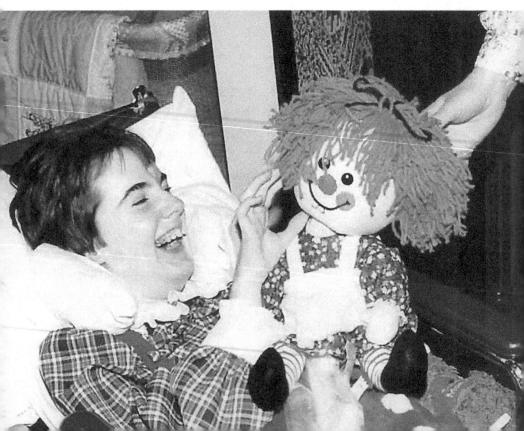

CHAPTER 8 **Fear of the Future**

Day 7
Thursday July 30

As far as I know things are on the upward swing with Annie. When I talk to
Mom this morning she says that Annie has eaten a couple of ounces of yogurt.
Whenever Mom manages to get Annie to keep down any little bit of nourishment,
it raises her spirits immensely and gives us all hope. But underneath the hope
I tally all the mountains Annie has to cross to recover from this and regain her
strength. My hope cannot shed enough light to illuminate the way forward, and
I am still afraid.

Although my parents first mentioned the idea of a feeding tube last weekend
before the crisis hit a peak on Tuesday, I haven't heard that idea being kicked
around much anymore. I'm not sure what that means. I'm still not sure where
I stand, but for now it's not an issue. Annie is way too weak to put her through
anything like that right now.

Since there is a limit to how much Annie is willing to swallow, I still think that if
they can get an IV to help with the fluids, they will be able to concentrate her

swallowing efforts on nutrition. But again, we don't know if an IV would even be a viable option for her. Right now things are on an even keel.

I'll call Mom later and see how the day has gone. I'm planning to go to Dayton tomorrow.

1975

Senior year in high school I had Mr. McDonald for health class. He was a short but stocky middle-aged man. A power-packed dynamo. He was also the head varsity football coach. Everybody was intimidated by him. He never smiled, and I witnessed him on occasion swatting the football players over the head with his clipboard as he strutted around the sidelines having fits.

Senior year of high school in Mr. McDonald's health class we did group reports.

I have no recollection now of what my own health report was about all those years ago, or anyone else's for that matter, except for one. I remember two things about that day: one group's report on mental retardation, and that I was reading Ayn Rand's *Atlas Shrugged* at the time. At one point I was hoping *Atlas Shrugged* would save me. I was hoping *Atlas Shrugged* would transport me away to another place and time where I wouldn't hear what was said in that classroom and where the sharp fingers of reality would not puncture the fragile place I kept safely buried inside.

The group of three presenters went to the front of the room, stood behind the podium with their notes in hand, and started talking about mental retardation. When they got to the part about the various categories or degrees of mental retardation and started using terms like "idiot" and "imbecile," I raised my hand.

In a voice that I'm sure wasn't as calm as I was striving to make it sound, and not completely free of the sharp edge of irritation, I asked, "Are they still using those names? Don't you think families of children with mental retardation would find this offensive?"

Coach McDonald looked up from the stack of papers he had been perusing at his desk by the door. The presenting group made some kind of conciliatory remark, and an unspoken message circulated around the room. "Uh oh. Her sister has brain damage." Everyone knew my sister had brain damage, except maybe Coach McDonald.

The presenting group then went on to explain the various difficulties that families had to face or overcome when they had a member with brain damage. And I recognized the warning signs of a thickening in my throat and a welling up behind my eyes. I decided to ignore the whole report and the three presenters. I opened *Atlas Shrugged*, without concern for repercussions from Coach McDonald, and began to read.

From the front of the room the words forced their way in, "Parents worry about what will happen to their child as they grow older."

I re-read the paragraph and tried to drown out the voices with the typed words on the now blurry page.

"Will they still be able to take care of their child as they grow old?"

I turned the page and tried again to focus my thoughts on Dagny Taggart's railroad crisis.

"What will happen to the child when the parents die?"

That was it. It was over. I lost it. Try though I did, I just could not hold back the flow of tears. Three pairs of eyes from the front of the room immediately zoomed in on me, and six feet began to shuffle. The speaker stopped in mid-sentence, and a hush fell over the room. I stood up and picked up my books. With my head bent and my eyes on the ground, I silently walked to the back of the room, around the desks, right past Coach McDonald, and out the door.

1970s | *Mom, Carol, Annie, me and Dad at a holiday celebration.*

'Twas Grace that taught my heart to fear,
And Grace my fears relieved.

How precious did that Grace appear
The hour I first believed.

CHAPTER 9

Ancestral Angels

Day 8

Friday July 31

Although Mom thinks Annie is on the mend, Carol is not so optimistic when I talk to her on the phone. I try to rationally look at the facts, and I think Annie is still in big trouble. I keep remembering how Annie started throwing up before this whole episode started in June, and we really still don't know why. I remember that first phone call from Carol about Dad's dream that Annie died, and I think about how emaciated Annie looks. I can't shake this feeling of impending doom that hangs over my head like a dark ominous cloud.

I do not know how my mother will survive if Annie dies. Like Dr. Ryan said, I know we all have to die someday, but in all my pleadings with God to be merciful with determining the end of the highly interdependent trio made up of my mom, my dad and Annie, I have come to the conclusion that this option of Annie dying first was the least desirable scenario. My parents have cared for her and nurtured her most of their adult lives. They have built their lives around her and they love her with both joy and desperation.

How do you let go of such a dependent child? I believe that if heaven does exist we all exist there in perfect forms. I'm buying into the whole package—the blind shall see, the deaf shall hear, the lame will walk and the mute will speak. If Annie does die, I believe she will leap for joy in the afterlife, if there is an afterlife. I believe if such a place does exist, Annie will be dancing in heaven.

Even so, I can't bear the idea of letting her slip away to a place where there is no one to look out for her, where none of us are. Worse yet, how do my parents surrender the care of this so special child into a heaven where they won't be? I know this thought process is contradictory, but what I want to believe, what I believe, and what I know to be true are all different and at times elusive concepts that cross back and forth over each other in my mind. At some core level I am afraid that Annie will not know where to go or what to do if she gets to heaven.

Then I remember that three of my grandparents have gone before us. And I know that if there is a God and a heaven and souls in heaven, then my grandparents are there watching over us. I know that they will embrace Annie in their arms. I find some kind of comfort in this idea. So I sit down at my computer and click through my files of family photographs until I come across the one of my mom's father holding Annie in his arms beside my grandmother. Then I find the one where my dad's mother is sitting on the sofa with Carol and Annie in her arms. I print out both photos then walk down the stairs to the basement where I locate the box of unused, or recyclable picture frames. I brush the cobwebs off of two that are the perfect size and place the fresh family prints in them.

When I arrive in Dayton I go straight into Annie's room and hand the photos to Mom. "Annie has these angels watching over her," I say. Mom smiles and chuckles. "Yes, she does," she says as she stands the photos on Annie's dresser. My mom is probably thinking these ancestral angels will help Annie get better, while I am thinking these angels will watch over Annie when she gets to heaven.

2009

In the spring, as we were working through the DDS steps required to approve caregivers for Annie, our caseworker Rob came over one afternoon to fill out Annie's DDS individualized service plan. My parents sat in the two wing-backed chairs in front of the large picture window in the living room while Rob sat across the room on the sofa. I was sitting in the wooden rocker close to Annie. Even though Rob understood the extent of Annie's disabilities, he went through the litany of questions one by one to fill in the questionnaire he was required to complete. And one by one my mom answered, "No."

"Can Diane schedule her medical appointments?"

"No."

"Can Diane eat or drink without assistance?"

"No."

"Can Diane brush her teeth without assistance?"

"No."

"Can Diane dress herself?"

"No."

Even though I knew how limited Annie's abilities were, it became painful for me to continue to listen to them listed in such a comprehensive and detailed fashion. I thought about all the other DDS clients who maybe *could* brush their teeth or feed themselves. I wanted to say, "No, she can't brush her own teeth, but she can cross her fingers when requested to do so, if she feels like it. She can understand that when she hears the 'pop' of the baby food jar she is going to get dinner soon." I wanted to say, "She can use her thumb to twirl her ring around on her finger." I want to tell him every little thing that she can do, but I don't. I sit silently and listen to the litany of questions and my mom's "no."

When Rob started probing Annie's communication abilities, I spoke up and said I would personally like to see an effort made to try to train Annie to communicate. I always believed it was possible that she could learn to use a communication device of some kind, and over the years I purchased different tools of communication—picture cards, a two-button yes or no device—to no avail. I simply wasn't able to get to Dayton frequently enough to be able to work with Annie on it, and my parents were reluctant. My mom said it caused Annie to have seizures if she had to concentrate or focus on something for too long.

The other problem I have to acknowledge is that from the beginning Mom had hopes for Annie that were systematically dashed one by one over the years. At some point Mom refused to set herself up for any more disappointments with Annie. She stopped trying new ideas. No more tests, no more exercises, no more walkers, and no more school buses. At some point my parents settled and stopped trying to improve the situation but adopted the approach of doing the best they could do on their own. They found life with Annie was easiest if they tried not to rock the boat.

But I hadn't suffered all the dashed hopes and disappointments like my parents had. I think that was partly why my mom wasn't particularly excited about the idea of Annie communicating, while it was an almost unbearable hope of mine.

Rob wrote in his notes:

"Diane communicates through gestures, facial cues and eye contact."

Rob developed two basic goals for Annie to work on: indicating a preference, and assisting with bathing.

Her skill development on her service plan read as follows:

> "Staff will offer two activities for Diane to choose from. Staff will state each activity with plenty of time between options. Staff will then ask Diane which activity she would like. Staff will again state each activity, encouraging Diane to give a positive response (a smile, laugh or vocalization). Staff can introduce a picture board, as Diane is able to tolerate, to facilitate Diane's communication. Examples of activities that can be offered to Diane include, but are not limited to: being read to, being sang to, watching a movie/TV, listening to the radio, etc. Staff will praise Diane for her participation in selecting an activity. Staff will monitor Diane for pre-seizure activity during this goal, as Diane has gone into seizures when focusing on something for too long."

Her second goal read as follows:

> "Staff will assist Diane with preparation of her washcloth with soap. Staff will place washcloth in Diane's right hand and will ask Diane to bring the washcloth to her left arm. Staff will gently place their hand over Diane's hand and will assist Diane with washing the top part of her left arm."

In truth, we were looking for help with Annie's care more than developing her abilities. So when Rob started talking about some of these goals, it was a little painful for me. What if she really could be trained to communicate and we hadn't worked with her enough to enable that for her? I couldn't bear to imagine how that possibility might have changed her life.

My parents actually did develop their own form of communication with Annie. Mom paid close attention to her preferences. She said the first time she realized Annie liked certain music, they were driving in the car and Annie got very excited. "What in the world is she getting excited about?" Mom asked. And then it dawned on her that an Elvis Presley song was playing on the radio. It was the first time she made the connection that there were certain songs Annie liked. "It came as a complete surprise to me," Mom said. Annie could recognize a song she liked from just a very few notes.

If you asked Annie if she was tired and wanted to go to bed, she learned to close her eyes in response. I also think Annie communicated to my parents through non-verbal ways that were more extensive than anyone else ever realized. But the possibility of her being able to communicate more specifically and universally to others was something that felt like a big balloon expanding inside of me on the verge of bursting. I feared to hope.

1958 | Our grandma holds Carol and Annie.

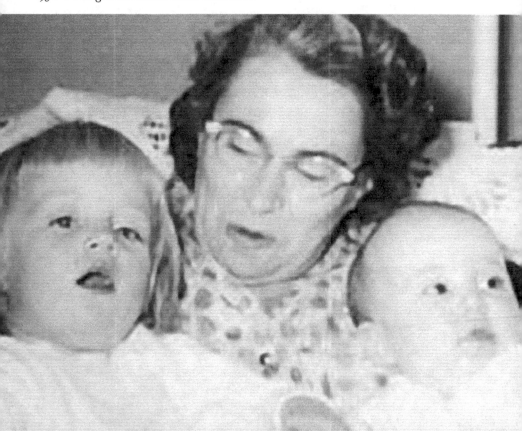

CHAPTER 10 **The ER**

Day 9
Saturday August 1

I make my usual morning phone call to Dayton today and find out from Carol, who answers the phone, that things really are basically the same. Unlike phone conversations I've had over the past few days with my mother who has been guardedly, or perhaps determinedly, optimistic, Carol thinks Annie is slipping away. Mom is refusing to take phone calls again because she is either too tired or unwilling to leave Annie's side for any period of time. I don't plan to come to Dayton today. I feel helpless, useless, and anxious as if my hands and legs are tied and I am witness to an impending train wreck but unable to take a step, call out a warning, or do anything about it.

In the evening my husband Mark and I attend a birthday party for Mark's sister Kathy's husband, our brother-in-law Tom. The party is being held at Tom's brother's house in the back yard with the garage door open and the food set up on tables within. It is a beautiful warm evening, and there is a compartmentalized part of me that can appreciate that, but I still am unable to fully participate in the celebratory spirit of the event. I am sick with worry, and my mind and heart are in Dayton with my parents and Annie.

While I am standing near the open garage door entrance and filling my plate with appetizers, one of Tom's relatives, Colleen, comes in to talk to me. Colleen is just a few years older than me. She is tall and thin with warm brown eyes and short brown hair. The freckles that cover her face give her a youthful appearance. Over the years I have seen and spoken to Colleen at Kathy and Tom's family celebrations like graduations and weddings. Colleen is a nurse, and she has a quiet tone of voice and calm demeanor. She exudes care and concern with her comments.

"Kathy told me about your sister Annie," Colleen says. "I've been praying for her. How is she doing?"

I feel comfort and distress at the same time—comfort that my sister-in-law has called for prayers as help for Annie, and distress that she thinks Annie needs prayers. It is bigger than me and out of my hands. I feel as if I am being swept away on a wave with no ability to guide my path.

"Annie's skin looks very pale, almost gray," I say, desperate to glean some kind of medical insight or diagnosis from a remote evaluation. "Her mouth droops at one side. Do you think it's possible she's had a stroke?" I ask.

"It can be a sign of a stroke," Colleen says, "But a drooping mouth can sometimes be a sign of dehydration."

I feel a small sense of relief. I think dehydration is the more likely explanation; so hopefully Annie has not had a stroke. I also feel even more frustrated that I have, as yet, been unable to find a way to get Annie an IV.

These feelings are replaced by a deeper and more solid sense of doom when I arrive home later in the evening and listen to a message on my answering machine from my sister. My parents have taken Annie to the emergency room. The hospital was going to admit Annie and they were waiting to find a room with two empty beds so that Mom could stay with her.

I will find out later from Annie's medical records that at the time of her arrival in the ER, her white blood cell count was 23,000 or more than twice the high end of the typical range; her platelets were elevated at 1,337,000 which is nearly four times the normal level; and her hemoglobin was 8.9 compared to the typical 12–16 gm/dL for women. Although no one mentioned this to us at the time, during her physical examination Annie was described as looking pale and cachetic or having the "wasting syndrome." The definition of cachexia (according to Mosby's Medical Dictionary, 8th edition. © 2009, Elsevier.) is, "General ill health and malnutrition, marked by weakness and emaciation, usually associated with severe disease, such as tuberculosis or cancer." Of course, we know none of this at the time; only that Annie has a high white blood count and low hemoglobin.

I don't know how long Annie will be in the hospital. Because of the effects of my dad's dementia, in particular his loss of good judgment at times, he should not be left alone at home or anywhere else really. Someone should be with Mom as well.

I pack an overnight bag with enough clothes to spend a couple of nights in Dayton, put my pajamas on, lie down in bed, and try to go to sleep.

May 2002

In the spring of 2002, I suffered with a lot of neck pain, made significantly worse by a jostling jeep ride through the desert of Sedona, Arizona to view native cliff dwellings. The pain ran down my left arm, and the only relief I could find was to raise my arm and rest my forearm on my head. Seeing no other recourse, I visited a neurosurgeon Dr. Shennan and had an MRI.

On a Wednesday, I went to Dr. Shennan's office for the MRI results. When he clipped the films up on his light board it became immediately apparent to me that something was out of line in my neck. Even with my untrained eye, I could clearly see a bulge between two of the vertebrae. Dr. Shennan pointed out what I had already seen for myself and told me I had a herniated disc, but that the good news was he could fix it with surgery.

I had gone to see Dr. Shennan hoping to be able to get physical therapy that would correct my problem. I had had a similar, although not nearly as severe, neck problem in the past that was cured by a trip to a physical therapist and exercises to do at home.

"Maybe I can just have physical therapy," I suggested. I did not sign up for neck surgery and was feeling very scared about the idea.

Dr. Shennan did not entertain the idea of therapy for even a moment. "The disc is pressing on your nerve. Eventually the pain will go away on it's own," he said. "At that point you will lose the use of your arm."

Dr. Shennan was a very busy man due to his highly respected reputation in our community. My mother-in-law had to wait over a month just to get an appointment to see him, so my anxiety level shot up when he told me I could schedule the surgery for two days later, on Friday. He explained that they would cut through the front of my throat, remove the offending disc, and replace it with a custom-made one he would harvest from my hip bone and sculpt to fit.

Fright doesn't come close to describing what I was feeling. I was downright terrified at the prospect of having my neck slit. But thankfully, things happened pretty rapidly. The earth kept revolving; the sun rose and set, and the next thing I knew I was in a hospital gown signing forms notifying me of all the possible consequences of the procedure, paralysis and death being the two that stuck out the most in my mind.

As I was waiting in the hospital room with my husband the day of the surgery, I was a nervous wreck, beside myself with worry, and ready to take any relaxation aids the next nurse who passed my way could provide. I was completely preoccupied with myself and what was going to happen to me.

Then I heard a commotion and familiar voices in the hallway outside my open door. The next moment my parents surprised me by walking into my room, pushing Annie in front of them. I had no idea they were planning to come.

My attention immediately shifted to Annie. I could tell she was responding with curiosity and interest to the unusual atmosphere of a hospital room and me in bed in a hospital gown. I immediately greeted her in a strong and cheerful voice, "Hey, Annie! Where are you? What are we doing in this place?" I was sharply aware at the time that she made me momentarily forget myself and my problems. I suspect she has done that to one extent or another the entire time I was growing up beside her.

2006 | *Mom, Dad and Annie pose for a photo.*

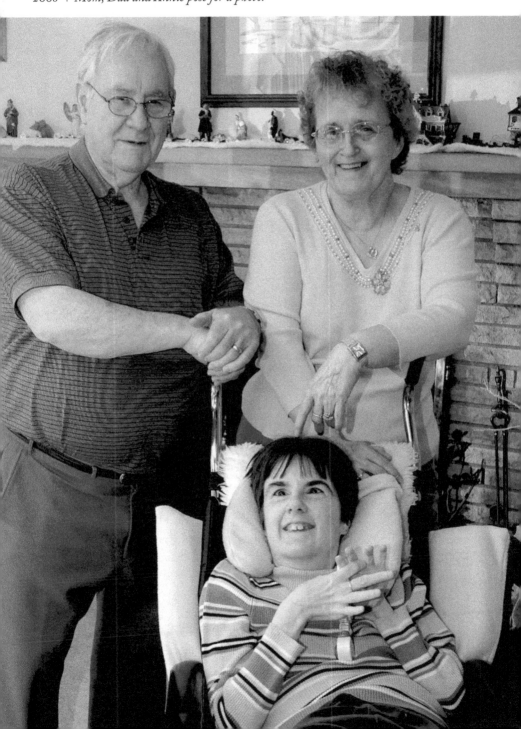

CHAPTER 11 The Oncology Floor

Day 10
Sunday August 2

I am on the road to Dayton by 7:30 a.m. I want to get to the hospital in time to hear what Annie's doctor has to say when he makes his rounds. My experience with Mark's parents over their many hospital stays, because of one illness or another, has taught me that doctors typically visit the patients early in the morning. If you aren't there, you miss the opportunity to ask questions and find out what is going on. Annie is in a different hospital, in a different city than Mark's parents were, but I believe things are probably the same.

Annie is on the fifth floor, and as I exit the elevator I notice that she is actually on the oncology floor. I dismiss this fact as interesting but without significance; she is here because this is the floor where the room with two available beds is located so that Mom can stay overnight with her.

Mom is up, dressed, and has made her bed by the time I arrive. When I ask, she says she was able to sleep a little through the night. I tell her I called Carol this morning and she is planning to bring Dad over to the hospital after he gets his shower and has breakfast. All of this is fine with Mom. Her focus of concern is honed in on Annie who is awake and lying on her stomach in her bed.

Mom tells me that she had to talk the nurse into letting Annie sleep on her stomach. Annie's vital signs are being monitored through a series of wires clipped to stickers on her body. Initially the stickers were placed on her stomach and chest, as is done for all patients who have to sleep on their backs while wearing them. Annie always sleeps on her stomach and will not go to sleep on her back. Mom explained this to the nurse and asked if the monitors could be placed on her back for the night. The nurse wasn't sure the monitor would work that way, but she agreed to try. So together Mom and the nurse unclipped the wires from the front but left the stickers in place, then turned Annie over onto her stomach, added stickers to her back and hooked her up. The nurse was concerned that the monitors wouldn't sense and record Annie's heart rate as well in this position, so she left the room and went to the nurses' station to check. Because Annie is so thin, everything worked out okay, and both Annie and Mom were able to sleep. In my mind I say a prayer of thanksgiving for a room with two hospital beds and a nurse willing to work with my mom.

All I know at this point is that there is something unusual or wrong with Annie's blood, and that they are giving her morphine for pain. But having watched Annie's decline over the past days, I do not have a lot of hope that this is going to end well. I look at my mother who has that artificial early morning freshness that happens when you haven't had enough sleep but need to start a big day early anyway. She is being strong and brave.

The nurse comes in to turn Annie back over onto her back, and Mom helps her reattach all the monitor wires. Even with the IV, Annie's face still looks pale, and although her spirits seem lifted a bit, she is not smiling and is nowhere near her usual responsive self.

True to my prediction, my parents' physician, Dr. Richards, walks into Annie's room a little after 9:00 a.m. He explains that Annie's white blood cell count and platelettes are both extremely high. Her red blood cell count at 7.6 is dangerously low. Dr. Richards talks about giving Annie a blood transfusion. He is looking at three possibilities right now for what could be wrong with her—leukemia, gall bladder disease, or pancreatitis. Dr. Richards says they are going to schedule some tests and that he has called a hematologist in to see her.

I start analyzing the different possibilities and weighing the options in my mind. I'm not sure what we will do if it is leukemia, but I've known people who were able to survive it by taking medicine.

Gall bladder disease is prevalent in our family. My mom and aunt both had their diseased gall bladders removed surgically. Surgery is not really an option for Annie. When we were young, Carol and I had our tonsils removed after bouts with tonsillitis, but the doctors refused to operate on Annie when she got tonsillitis. A doctor told my Mom that there wasn't a doctor in the country who would touch it because of Annie's situation. It would be extremely dangerous, and no one wanted to take a chance on it. This is the same story Mom and Dad have heard over the years whenever any kind of medical condition came up with Annie. No one wanted to put her under a general anesthetic for any reason.

I don't have any idea what pancreatitis is, or what is involved in its treatment, so I ask Dr. Richards. He says that typically pancreatitis requires a treatment of rest for the digestive system. I'm not sure what all is involved, but to me it seems like the most favorable diagnosis. I start praying that Annie has pancreatitis.

Mom says, "Leukemia is the one I'd be most worried about."

"You shouldn't be," Dr. Richards says. "The gall bladder is the bigger risk. According to the doctors I've consulted with, it would be futile to try to operate with the situation her stomach is in."

Dr. Richards looks at Mom and says, "I want you to take a break this afternoon and go home for a while."

Carol and Dad show up shortly after Dr. Richards leaves. My mom is sitting in a chair under the large window at the far side of the room, beside the bed she slept in. Annie is in the bed closest to the door. Outside the window a metal structure of construction in progress across the street occupies most of the view. Dad sits down in the chair beside Mom, and she turns and leans towards him. She recounts what Dr. Richards has just told us. "What are we going to do if it is her gall bladder?" she asks. Dad has no answer.

Carol doesn't stay long. Meanwhile, it seems like people are trying, and not always able, to get blood from Annie every couple of hours or so. It is painful for me to watch Annie's face as they stick her with needles. This is torture. A nurse has informed us that a picc line has been ordered for Annie. Once it is in they will be able to get blood and administer medicines through it without having to stick Annie every time. This sounds like a great plan to me, although I am a little nervous about what is involved in the actual insertion of the picc line.

I start standing guard fiercely. When lab techs come in the room with a needle, I tell them that Annie is scheduled to get a picc line and they need to wait for that. Sometimes I am able to scare them away.

At lunchtime I tell my parents that they should go take a break in the cafeteria together and I will stay with Annie. My parents leave, and I sit down in the chair by Annie's side.

My parents have been gone close to an hour when a tall distinguished man enters the room and introduces himself as Dr. Shien, the hematologist. He starts to explain what he thinks about Annie's blood levels when I interrupt him. I think he should be telling my mom and dad this, so I say, "Her mother should be back any minute now," hoping he will wait. He looks a bit confused when I tell him I am her sister. He returns to the hall and rechecks Annie's chart. I suspect he has mistaken me for Annie's mother.

People often mistake Annie for being much younger than she is. Mom said that when they are out in public sometimes people will ask them if Annie is their grandchild. She doesn't look her age. She is small in stature and she's been protected from the physical stresses of the environment, like the sun. More importantly, she has led an emotionally stress-free life as far as we can tell. Her face hasn't aged much and unlike my graying hair, hers has remained a deep brown color.

Fortunately Mom does return within minutes, and Dr. Shien tells us that Annie needs a blood transfusion. He writes the orders for it on Annie's chart and leaves.

Mom is worried about giving Annie a blood transfusion. She has heard stories and is fearful about contaminated blood. She worries about exposing Annie to HIV or hepatitis. Mom calls Dr. Richards, whom she trusts, just to make sure he thinks it will be all right.

Carol returns and takes Mom and Dad home in the afternoon while I stay with Annie, but Mom comes back after only a couple of hours.

"I couldn't take a nap," she says, "and it makes me nervous wandering around the house with nothing to do. I am more comfortable and relaxed here."

This hospital visit so far has done absolutely nothing to allay my fears for Annie.

I take Mom to the cafeteria for dinner. We're sitting across from each other at the institutional table in the stark and brightly lit cafeteria, with our trays littered with crumpled napkins, mostly empty plates, and used silverware. We are finishing up our beverages when I make eye contact with Mom.

I am afraid Annie is dying. I am afraid my mom is going to be crushed into dust if Annie does die. I want my mom to be able to survive the blow I believe is coming. I don't know how to help her, but can only hope she is strong enough to help herself. "I think you'd better start preparing yourself," I tell her.

She looks at me and her eyes glaze over with tears, but none fall. "Annie may be out of miracles," she says. My eyes respond with tears that mirror hers. Her comment strikes me like a burst of light on her past, illuminating how she has lived these fifty-one years with fear followed by relief of near misses with Annie's health. Mom had a large party when Annie turned thirty. She had the birthday cake decorated with the words, "Annie made it to 30. Mom survived too." Mom probably saw each one of Annie's birthdays as a miracle. And I guess Annie's 51 years are miraculous when you consider doctors predicted she'd have a life expectancy of eight years, when she was initially tested and diagnosed as an infant. But I think Mom is right; Annie may be out of miracles.

When we're back in Annie's room after dinner, a young woman wearing a lab coat comes in. She has milk chocolate skin and long kinky curly hair pulled back into a bushy pony tail. She is carrying the tell-tale plastic handled bin of empty vials and rubber gloves.

"She is getting a picc line," I say. "The blood samples are supposed to wait until after the picc line is in."

"This is a 'stat' order," the lab tech replies as she walks over to the table near me and sets her bin down. "I have to take it now." Then she walks over to Annie and examines her hands. "Did someone else already try to take blood out of her today?"

"Yes. The last person stuck her twice and still was not able to get enough so she left."

She looks at my mom and says, "I told you last night to ask for me if someone came for blood today. I've done this fifteen years, and I was able to get all the blood we needed from her with one quick stick when she came in."

This was true. I had heard the story from my mom.

The lab tech comes back to the table for her supplies and goes back to Annie's side to work on getting the blood samples she needs. True to her word, she is able to get five or six vials out. She stands at the table with her back to me as she finishes up labeling the vials and says, "I was watching the orders for her name. When I saw 'Diane Smith' I took all the orders and came up." She stops what she was doing, turns to look me in the eyes and says, "She reminds me of my niece."

"Is she like Annie?" I ask.

"She was," she says.

"I'm sorry."

Tears fill her eyes and she explains, "She was only 11. I wish we could have had her with us as many years as you've had Annie." Then she swipes at her eyes and adds, "We are not supposed to do this."

"It's alright," I say.

I don't worry about the tears sliding down my face. I'm allowed to cry.

I go back home to my parents' house where Carol and I momentarily lose Dad who has walked outside in the dark. It's about 10 o'clock and Carol and I are on the driveway debating the necessity of knocking on neighbors' doors when we hear voices coming from the alley behind the house. Dad had wandered a few doors down, and the man who lives there is walking him back home. As Carol has had primary responsibility for Dad since Annie's been in the hospital, she determines not to let him out of her sight. "I don't want to be the one who loses Dad while Mom and Annie are at the hospital," she says.

Dad sits in the family room with me before he goes to bed. He reclines in the corner of the loveseat, leaning on the arm, with one leg stretched out on the cushions and the other folded in front of him. He looks so tired. I'm sitting close-by on the chair at the desk where I plan to send out a few e-mails to family and friends. I've started asking friends to pray for whatever is best. It is clear Dad has something on his mind he wants to talk about.

"I think my girl is in trouble," he says.

I turn away from my computer to face him. "I think she is in trouble too," I respond. "I wish I didn't have to say that, but I think she is in trouble."

"I had a dream I went to her funeral," Dad tells me. "I don't ever want to see that day."

I know that Dad is haunted by this dream as he has told me about it two or three times now. When Annie first got sick Carol said, "I don't know what will happen to Mom and Dad if Annie dies. No one can really understand the love and devotion they have for Annie." At the time I was overcome with my own worry and grief at the thought of losing this precious sister of mine. I said, "Right now I'm worried about me. I'm worried about *my* loss."

Now, as I sit and look at my dad's worry-worn face, I realize that I have to be strong enough to not only bear my own sorrow, but to try to support my parents as they bear what can only be a much greater sorrow. My dad seems to have lost his ability to use his intellect to help him deal with his emotions. In some ways he seems to behave like an innocent child that you want to protect from the harsh cruel realities of life. It is crushingly painful to have so many people I love suffering so much.

Although I desperately want to, I can't give Dad reassurance that everything will be okay. I don't believe everything will be okay. I struggle to find words that might at least provide some small amount of comfort. I tell him what gives me comfort. "She won't have to lose you," I say. Over the years I've worried now and then about how Annie would cope if Mom or Dad died. How would she understand when they were just gone? How do you explain death to a person like Annie?

"I don't want to see the day where you are gone and she is waiting for you to come home," I say. "If you have to suffer the loss of her, she won't be the one left behind here. She won't have to suffer the loss of you."

My words don't seem to bring my dad any solace. I don't know whether he can't fully comprehend what I am trying to tell him because of his Alzheimer's, or if he is just overcome with fear and grief. There is nothing more I can do.

I am afraid, too.

late 1950s to present

My dad told me that when they found out the way Annie was he thought, "She's one of the group." And my parents treated her as such, with the obvious things that had to be accounted for. "At the time, we made the decision that she was a full-fledged member of the family with a few more limitations than the rest," he said. "Everybody just had to learn to live with the situation the way it was."

My dad was insistent about including Annie in every aspect of our lives to the extent that was possible from holiday meals and family gatherings to cross-country vacations. She went with us everywhere our family went unless it was impossible for her to go.

Dad always wanted to travel and early in their marriage he worked a second job primarily because he wanted to earn extra money to buy a camper. Traveling, and particularly camping, with Annie introduced a lot of extra challenges. Mom said if it had been up to her, we probably wouldn't have ever gone anywhere.

Since Annie couldn't chew, she had to eat soft food. Dad told me that on a trip to Rochester, N.Y., when we stopped at a restaurant to eat, they weren't able to get a bowl of mashed potatoes and gravy to feed Annie. Mom and Dad put Annie on a standard diet of baby food after that, pretty much at my dad's insistence because baby food is available anywhere. On road trips he used to heat her baby food in its jar in a pan of water placed on the hot engine. We'd stop at a roadside park and Carol and I ran around the picnic tables while Mom and Annie sat in the car with the hood up and my dad 'cooked' her food.

My parents were usually able to take Annie wherever they wanted to go, although they had to overcome the obstacle of accessibility at their parish church in the early 80s. Usually my parents went to church separately, taking turns staying at home with Annie, but Mom was in the hospital recovering from surgery, so Dad took Annie to church with him. The church had not yet been renovated to become handicapped-accessible.

Dad placed Annie's wheelchair along the sidewall, but an usher started to move the wheelchair. So Dad moved Annie to the back of the church and placed her wheelchair along the back of the last pew where there was more room for it. The same usher came back and started adjusting the position of Annie's wheelchair again. I guess the usher still thought it was in the way and was trying to nudge it closer to the pew. I suspect it made Dad feel that

Annie wasn't completely welcome, or that she was an inconvenience and taking up space where she shouldn't have been.

Dad got upset and left the church with Annie. He put her back in the van, got in and drove around until the next Mass, when he was able to place Annie behind the last pew without incident.

The pastor, Father Joseph Reilly, witnessed the entire episode. After Mass, he approached Dad and asked about it.

Not long afterward, the church opened up a pew in the front to accommodate wheelchairs. Eventually, the remaining two front pews were opened up and a ramp was built.

After that, my parents took Annie with them to mass every Sunday. When my dad told me about the incident, he said, "I thought we needed to go as a family. She's just another parishioner."

Dad wanted Annie to have the fullest life possible. We have a vacation photograph of my dad sitting in sand where the beach met the waves. Annie is sitting in the sand in front of him, between his legs, as the water comes in and washes over them. In the photo he looks like he's enjoying the experience a lot more than Annie is.

Dad was Annie's constant protector and advocate—making sure she was not only safe, but also making sure she was included, concerned not only for her physical welfare, but also her enrichment.

Recently, Carol told me she saw him push Annie in her chair outside one night after dark to gaze up at a full moon in the summer sky.

1971 | Dad helps Annie experience the beach and waves on a vacation to Myrtle Beach.

CHAPTER 12 **A Picc Line**

Day 11
Monday August 3

Carol and I start to establish a comfortable routine. I get up and leave early to be at the hospital when the doctor comes, and Carol comes over later, taking her time and helping Dad get ready.

"I am not going to stay in the room when they do the picc line," I tell Carol before I leave for the hospital.

"None of us are," she says. "We are going to take Mom and leave the room for that procedure."

"Mom will want to stay and try to help Annie. It will be scary for her."

When I get to the hospital things are pretty much the same as they were yesterday. On the wall behind the head of Annie's bed, I glance at a recent photograph of her smiling. I took it over a year ago at my Dad's birthday party. I captured Annie smiling and looking right at me, which wasn't easy to do. She is holding her mirror and with a twinkle in her dark eyes, she looks energetic, vibrant and full of life. Now here in the hospital bed she just looks emaciated. Her skin is pale and her body is limp. Her eyes are dull, she is not smiling, and she lies quite still for the most part.

Yesterday I expressed my concern that, because of Annie's general condition of being disabled with brain damage, the people taking care of her in the hospital wouldn't realize that she doesn't usually look this way. I was afraid they would not realize how bad she is feeling. This may be true for most people who are hospitalized when they are not feeling like themselves, but for some reason it really bothered me that the nursing staff wouldn't know that Annie is normally a happy, smiling, loving little person. When Carol returned to the hospital yesterday, she brought back this picture of Annie smiling and taped it on the wall.

The contrast between the photo and Annie's strained face as she lies there is almost unbearable for me to see. I avoid looking at the photo.

Shortly after I arrive Father Maly, the current pastor of my parents' church, walks in the door. He greets my mother and asks her how things are going. He wants to know if we would like him to offer Annie the sacrament of the Anointing of the Sick. I say, "Yes" without hesitation, and Mom just goes along. In my heart I recognize the gravity of the situation and appreciate, on a gut level, the fact that the Catholic Church has changed the name of this sacrament from Last Rites to Anointing of the Sick. This allows me to pretend that Annie will recover, but also assures me that she will have received her last sacrament if this ends with her death.

Fr. Maly walks over to her bed and suggests that we hold hands. I am standing beside the bed by Annie's left arm that is bent up and resting on her chest as usual. I cover her left hand with my right hand and grasp my mom's hand with the other. Father Maly reads the prayers and asks us to say the Our Father with him. Our voices sound small and hollow during this quiet little ceremony in this room of metal railings, tubes, and hanging bags of fluid. The prayers take on a great significance, and I feel like it is of the utmost importance that I focus completely and intently on the words with all my mind, heart and soul. I want God to hear our small voices here beside Annie's bed. I want God to help her, if not to get better, then to get to heaven. When we finish I feel reassured and grateful that Annie has received this sacrament. I wish my dad could have been here for it.

When Dr. Richards arrives he tells us they are having trouble getting Annie's blood counts stabilized. He says that she came into the ER with a very low red blood count and that it continued to fall from 7.6 to 7.3 yesterday in the hours from 9:00 a.m. to 2:00 p.m. Now I understand why the lab techs came in a nearly constant stream to draw more blood and check her levels yesterday. He tells us she is scheduled for an ultrasound on her stomach and abdomen this morning to try to determine why she is having trouble eating and keeping food down. He says that not much is going to be happening for 24 to 48 hours until they get test results in. There may be a CT-scan soon, if the ultrasound is non-conclusive.

"Your best-case scenario is, if it *is* Annie's gall bladder and I can find a surgeon who is willing to do arthroscopic surgery on her," Dr. Richards says even though yesterday he told us that would be the worst case of what he thought were our three possibilities. Dr. Richards says we should be able to have a conversation about options tomorrow or the next day once the test results are in.

After Dr. Richards leaves, I ask the nurse what the red blood count should be, and she tells me that for a woman anything lower than 8.0 is considered critical. She also says that the IV Annie is getting could be partly responsible for the drop in numbers as the fluids dilute her blood. Once the picc line is in, Annie will be getting a blood transfusion tonight and tomorrow that should help.

Four hours later, the ultrasound has been done, and Mom and Dad are at lunch. I am leaning over Annie's bed with my back to the door and my forearms on the bed. I am resting my head against Annie's and singing to Neil Diamond playing from my iPod earphones placed on the pillow close to her ears. Yesterday I put her favorite music on my iPod for this purpose. I meant to bring my iPod speakers, but this morning I forgot them at Mom's house. This is working okay. Annie likes me being close to her. I bounce my hip to the beat and sing along. "Sweet Caroline, da da da , good times never seemed so good…"

There is a quick knock at the door and I jerk upright, startled. A man and woman in green scrubs come in with several pieces of equipment. They aren't smiling.

More than a little embarrassed, I turn off the I-pod, wrap up the earphones, and place it in my pocket.

"We're here to do the picc line," the man says.

I am expecting my parents back from the cafeteria any minute. I look at the door, but they aren't in sight, and now the door is nearly blocked with the equipment.

"Can I stay in here with her?" I ask after a brief hesitation. I am caught between wanting to escape and needing to be here for Annie.

"It's a sterile procedure," the man says, "you'll have to wait outside."

Even though I feel bad that Annie is going to have to go through this alone, I also feel a little relieved that I am not going to have to witness it.

I start to gather my things, my book and my purse, and ask, "Do you want to ask me anything about her before I leave?" They both look at me quizzically, but neither respond. "Well, if you need to ask me something, I will be right outside the room."

The man looks at Annie, looks back at me and says, "You can stay."

They hand me a yellow mask that I put over my nose and mouth, and I follow their directions when they tell me to go around to the other side of Annie's bed as they drape her with the sterile cloths. "Can I hold her hand?" I ask.

"Yes. Just try to stay under this blue cloth."

The man, who I think is a doctor, although I don't know for sure because he never introduced himself, explains to me that they have to put a local anesthetic on her arm and that it will burn. Then they have to use a needle that will hurt.

He takes Annie's right arm and says, "She'll have to let go of this bottle." When Annie first got sick, Mom put a glass bead in the bottom of a plastic baby bottle that she now holds most of the time. If Annie gets upset she waves her right arm around violently, and we can hear the bead. It helps us know how she's feeling. Annie doesn't, however, willingly give up anything that she is holding in her right hand. I gently pry her fingers from the bottle and place it on the bed beside her. "You're going to get this back soon, Sweetheart," I say.

The man takes her right arm and begins to tape it down to the table so it will be immobile. I grimace that she can't use her right arm anymore, which is a large means of her communication. I just want to get this procedure over with as fast as possible.

My glasses begin to fog up. I look at the man who is also wearing a mask and glasses and ask him, "How do you keep your glasses from fogging up?" His eyes smile and he says, "You have to pinch it at the nose a little."

I try, but there is nothing to pinch. "You have it on upside-down," the nurse says. I can see they are both amused, but at least they are not laughing at me out loud.

"Well that's a fine note," I say to Annie. "I've got my mask on upside-down." She smiles a little at the inflection in my voice.

With my left hand holding hers under the blue cloth, I lean over the bed placing my face beside hers and talk to her through the entire procedure. "You're a good girl," I tell her. "You're brave." When the doctor gives me a warning, I say, "This is going to hurt a little, Sweetheart." And then I offer up an audible "Ouch," for her when she jerks and her lips tighten and she starts blowing her cheeks out. "You're doing so good," I say.

The man explains that the picc line will enter the upper arm and push through a vein all the way into the chest. I try not to watch what the doctor is doing too closely, but just keep Annie's eyes and attention on me. "The worst part is over now," he says.

I keep up the chatter. "This is going to make you feel better," I say to Annie.

"He is helping you.

"You are doing good.

"I'm going to give you your bottle back soon."

I see a surprisingly long, thin wire in the man's gloved hands that looks pretty scary to me. "She's going to feel some pressure now," he says.

Annie's face responds as he starts threading the wire into her arm. "Oh, oh, oh," I say for her. He stops feeding the wire in and she relaxes.

I look up at him and ask, "Were you able to get it in?"

"Yes. It will work."

I collapse onto the mattress beside Annie's little body as the tears pour out of my eyes, and I audibly sob. I don't want her to see, but I can't stem the onslaught. No one says anything. I pull myself together and start back up the chatter as they finish up. The man leaves the room. The woman seems kind as she says, "Why don't you turn off the light over her head so it doesn't glare into her eyes." And she leaves the room.

2006

When I first decided to interview my parents for a story I wanted to write about Annie for the Feature Writing class I was taking at a nearby college, it seemed like a good idea. But as the day approached, I began to realize I had serious trepidation, and as my husband Mark and I drove up I-75 on our way to see my parents, I was downright nervous. Although Annie had been a part of my life for forty-eight out of my forty-nine years at the time, for some reason I felt very anxious about having this conversation about her with my parents. I suppose I knew that the vulnerable, painful, place deep inside of me that holds a whole confused mix of emotions was about to be probed once again.

In my interview I wanted to find out what this meant to my parents as they looked back over their lives. I wanted to understand how they managed to cope with the care of a disabled child, even into their seventies. I wanted to know how they dealt with the imposed restraints on their lives and their freedom to come and go and pursue their own interests. I wanted to hear their perspective of how having a disabled sibling affected my other sister and me, and what they might do differently if they were starting over. I was expecting to hear a lot about the personal sacrifices they made over the years, some that I witnessed and many that I did not.

When we arrived at my parents' house Dad was just finishing up feeding Annie, so I settled into the dining room to wait. Mark went into the family room where he would keep Annie company, and I pulled a notebook and small cassette recorder from my tote bag and placed them on the dining room table. I sat on one side, my mom was to my left at the head of the table and when my father joined us, he sat directly across from me. I was well prepared with questions,and I asked my first one.

"Were there things you wanted to do while you were raising us, with us or for us, that you weren't able to do because of Annie?" I asked.

"A lot of them," Mom replied immediately. This conversation led to a discussion of family vacations that we took and the time we went to Old Man's Cave. "Dad carried her," Mom said. "That was a hard job. There was no way of getting her in there other than carrying her."

I looked at her, a little surprised, because even though I remember going to Old Man's Cave, I didn't remember that Dad carried Annie the whole way. I asked her what seemed like an obvious question, "What were we doing at Old Man's Cave with Annie?"

"Dad was the motivator," Mom said. "There were probably a lot of places I wouldn't have gone if it had been up to me. I would have taken the easy way out and said, 'We can't go there. That's going to be too much trouble.' And it was trouble. You had so much extra stuff and different things you had to think about when you had a handicapped child who couldn't eat regular food. It was a lot of trouble."

"But you were willing to do it," I noted.

"Yeah," Mom said, "So that you would be able to go."

I really wanted to probe the idea of what my parents sacrificed, or what, perhaps, my sister and I missed out on because of Annie. "So you thought about the fact that you had nondisabled children that had needs," I said, "Was that a big part of your thinking process?"

"Only that we would try to fit her in the best that she would fit in and try to do things that we would normally do if she wasn't there," Mom said.

I continued to try to probe and get my parents to speak of the way they coped, but as the conversation went on it became increasingly clear that it was all about Annie. Her needs were foremost in their minds, not their own. I asked my Dad, "Do you have any regrets?"

He didn't say, "That I couldn't travel places I would have liked to." And I knew he would have liked to.

He didn't say, "That I was never free to come and go." Even though he and my mom were never free to come and go.

He didn't say, "That I never took a break from the day-in, day-out constancy of the care of your sister."

What he did say was, "The biggest regret I've got of the whole thing is that she cannot speak. Everything else I can deal with pretty much as it comes along."

I was struggling with my emotions at this point in the conversation. I was overcome by the amount of love for, and devotion to, Annie they were expressing. Even though I had grown up witnessing it all my life, I was moved by how selfless they were. I was fighting back the tears, but I was still holding my own. "How do you think our lives would have been different as a family if she would have not been disabled?" I asked. "Well, I'd have had one more bright daughter," Dad said. The tears welled up in my eyes, and my throat thickened, but I managed to regroup, fight it back, and maintain my composure.

My parents did say they regretted not keeping up with Annie's physical exercises they had tried when she was young. It took a lot of time and people and I think they just eventually gave up on it. They regretted not continuing because it might have kept Annie's left leg and arm from becoming so stiff.

I tried to suggest that they might be able to get Annie into physical therapy, even though she was in her late forties. I was still doing okay emotionally at this point and thinking that I was on fairly safe territory, until my dad responded, "At this stage of the game, I won't agree to anything that looks like it would cause her to be uncomfortable. The biggest fear I have is when I'm...," my dad's voice cracked here, and he stuttered slightly, "... not around to take care of her, is that she won't... I hope that at least she gets reasonable treatment, because I don't ever want anybody to hurt her."

That was it for me. I gave up my pretense. I was not going to be able to make it through this discussion without crying. I took my glasses off, placed them on the table, turned to my mother with tears running down my face and said, "I'm going to need some tissues."

My mom just laughed and said, "Okay. I'll get you some."

early 1970s | *Mom feeds Annie at a rest area on our way to a beach vacation.*

CHAPTER 13

Random Acts of Kindness

Day 12
Tuesday August 4

Today I need to have some basic maintenance done on my car, and I need to re-group. Yesterday I drove home to Cincinnati for dinner, to get more clothes, and to spend the night. I had hoped driving back to Cincinnati and putting distance between myself and Annie's hospital room might help reduce my stress levels. But my defenses have fallen, and instead of relief I feel exhaustion.

It is Mom and Dad's 55th wedding anniversary. I am going back to Dayton later this afternoon to participate in a small and quiet celebration we plan to hold in Annie's hospital room. Hopefully we'll know something more definitive about Annie's condition today. At the hospital they've talked to my mom about getting a nurse at home when Annie is released. So that is good.

After breakfast, I call my parents' house and find out from Carol the results from the ultrasound test Annie had done yesterday afternoon. The results are not conclusive, largely because none of Annie's internal organs are where they are supposed to be, probably due to the curvature of her spine. Mom already knew this was the case, because she stayed by Annie's side through the test and witnessed the technician struggling to find the internal organs he was trying to capture on the ultrasound. Mom also saw that the test was painful for Annie as her abdomen was prodded and she was moved around into different positions.

"The ultrasound indicated that there might be a mass in Annie's abdomen," Carol says.

"What do you mean a mass?" I ask. "What kind of mass?"

"I don't know," Carol answers. "They said it could possibly be her colon pushed up and out of position. They want to do a CT scan."

I take this news calmly. I have been in such an elevated state of panic and anxiety regarding Annie's condition that I am fairly numb right now. I believe any light the medical professionals can shed will help us understand what is going on and what we can do, or how we should proceed.

I don't have a lot of hope that Annie will be cured of what ails her. She has too many things wrong right now. Physically she is emaciated. She can't keep food down and really won't eat or drink. Her white blood count continues to skyrocket, and her red blood cells are depleted. Even if the blood transfusion she is scheduled to get today helps, what is to prevent her blood count from sliding back into this critical position? If what is wrong with her requires surgery, we are out of luck. It will be a miracle if we find a doctor willing to operate on her. Which may be a mute point, because my parents likely won't be willing to put Annie through it. My dad has always said, "I'm not going to let anyone cut on her." Annie's situation is bad.

I believe Annie is dying. I have felt this way for more than a week now.

Dr. Ryan's words on his first visit to our house to see Annie haunt me. "The day comes when every one of us has to die," he said.

If Annie dies, I just can't imagine what this loss would do to my parents. They have been devoted to her and have structured nearly every day of their entire married life together around her needs. I cannot imagine what my parents would look like coming to my home in their van, without lowering the electric lift and pushing Annie's wheelchair up the walk in front of them, my mom carrying a cooler of Annie's food and medicine.

I can't imagine family dinners without Annie positioned in her wheelchair close to the table. I can't fathom Christmas without standing by her side and helping her grasp the torn edge of wrapping paper I started so she could unwrap her gift. She loves the feel and the sound of paper as she pulls it off.

Will I momentarily forget as I walk into my parents' home and call out, "Annie, where are you?" Will I head for her bedroom to say goodbye when I am leaving? How do I shut down this sensor I have in my brain when I'm in her presence to check periodically to see if she looks comfortable or needs some kind of physical adjustment in her chair; to talk to her every now and then to keep her included in the conversation?

I drive back to Dayton after lunch and stop to pick my dad up before I go to the hospital. Carol is staying at the house because Mom had previously scheduled plumbers to come and replace an air conditioner. When I pull into the driveway, Dad is pushing Annie's empty wheelchair through the garage and around to the back of the van where the electric lift is.

Uh oh. I get out of my car and ask, "Why do you have Annie's chair, Dad?"

"I'm going to need it to bring her home," he says.

He doesn't know what he is doing. His Alzheimer's is making this whole ordeal so much harder on him, and as a result, on all of us.

"She's not coming home yet, Dad. Why don't you take her chair back in the house, and then I'll take you to the hospital."

Mark drives up in the late afternoon and stops to pick up a bucket of Kentucky Fried chicken and some side dishes to comprise a meal to celebrate my parents' anniversary in Annie's hospital room. Carol, Mark and I, and my parents are here.

We sit on the few chairs that are scattered in the room, or on the edge of the beds.

The dinner celebration is subdued. Annie actually looks pretty good today after the two blood transfusions she got last night and this morning. She has good color and is moving her right arm more. She also smiles easily again. She is excited that we are all here together. She loves a party.

Everyone leaves shortly after dinner except for Mom and me. Mark drives back to Cincinnati, and Carol takes Dad home. I stay with Mom for a little while because I have not spent a lot of time here in the last two days.

Before I leave to spend the night at my parents' house, a woman who is on the hospital's cleaning staff comes in the room. She empties the trashcans as she has done every day since we've been here. She always says something cheerful to Annie and tries to get her to laugh when she is in the room. Tonight after she finishes, she leaves and then comes back in the room with a small gift for Annie. It is a ceramic plaque about the size of a deck of cards and is inscribed with the words "Prayers are hopes with wings."

When I get back to my parents' house, I see Annie's wheelchair parked on an angle in front of the TV in the family room where she often sits.

"What is her wheelchair doing sitting there empty?" I ask Carol.

"Dad put it there."

"We've got to move it," I say. "I can't stand seeing it there empty."

Carol moves Annie's chair to a position against the wall in a corner of the living room. She lowers the elevated leg rests. Then she gets a colorful afghan and arranges it over the chair. Finally she places a stuffed animal in the chair. It is an adequate disguise.

through the years

My sister Annie, in her reclined wheelchair, was hard not to notice. Many times perfect strangers would come up to her and talk to her. Senator John Kerry was no exception. During the 2004 presidential campaign, democratic candidate Kerry happened to attend Mass at my parents' church. As they normally did, Mom and Dad had taken Annie with them to church. Because of Annie's wheelchair, they arrived early to get a seat up front in the handi-capped section. As a result, they were sitting right across the aisle from Kerry.

In the church, without the presence of cameras, Kerry stood up after Mass, walked over to Annie, leaned way down over her chair and said, "I just had to come over and say hello to you." Of course, Annie couldn't speak, so she gave no response—except for the large smile that she was so generous with.

Annie often brought out the best in people. As her family members, we were fortunate to have been witnesses of this. We were used to people not only being curious about Annie, but also being kind and generous to her.

A good example is the time we went to Cedar Point amusement park. Mom was pushing Annie in her wheelchair as we were walking through the game concourse, when a man came out of his booth and approached us. He asked my mom when Annie's birthday was. She told him May. He said, "Wait here just a minute," ran back into his booth, and returned with a little ceramic angel for the month of May. He said, "I wanted to give her something since she can't ride the rides."

Another time she got a huge stuffed Snoopy dog somewhere.

Friends and family acquaintances sometimes stopped by my parents' house with a small gift for Annie. Mom liked to talk about the people who came up to Annie and "acted like they've known her for ten years." An elderly man at church, after getting my parents' approval, regularly stopped on his way back from communion, as he walked past Annie, to lean over and kiss her on the forehead. Another man would also come over, lean down close to Annie's face and talk to her. She always just looked up and smiled. Annie was a magnet for random acts of kindness.

Before he retired my dad owned a tool & die shop, and my mom worked in the office taking Annie with her. One of Dad's customers was a college professor who always made a point of going into the office to say hello to Annie. During one of these visits the professor asked Mom if he could take Annie for a ride in his convertible. Mom was taken aback for a moment because she never took any risks where Annie was concerned. But on this particular day, for some reason, she agreed to let Annie go on the ride because she thought it would be fun for her. Annie always loved the wind in her face. They got Annie into the car, and the professor took her on a short ride. When they returned he said, "She smiled the entire time."

Sometimes when they took Annie out in public my parents would run into individuals who have Down syndrome. Dad said, "They are always affectionate towards her. They don't come up to me, but they come up to her."

People were not only curious, people wanted to make connections. "We find this a lot," Mom said. "If you're in a group of people, like at a festival somewhere, there are always people who will come up, and they've got a granddaughter, or a nephew, or somebody in their family who has a problem. It may not be exactly like Annie's, but they want to tell you what kind of a problem it is. It's just easy for them to talk to you about it."

1970s | Annie holds the Snoopy Dog, a gift from a stranger.

Through many dangers, toils and snares
I have already come;

'Tis Grace that brought me safe thus far
And Grace will lead me home.

CHAPTER 14 **Going Home**

Day 13
Wednesday August 5

We are expecting to get the results of Annie's CT scan today, and I want to be at the hospital early so I don't miss the doctor's visit. Carol is planning on helping Dad get ready and will bring him over a little later. She wants me to call her when we hear the test results.

My mom is sitting in a chair under the window beside the bed she sleeps in, and I am sitting in a chair beside Annie's bed when the doctor walks in her room. It is not Dr. Richards, but one of his associates, Dr. Donnelly. He is younger than Dr. Richards and is tall with light colored hair and a boyish face. He stands at the foot of Annie's bed and tells us he has the CT scan results. Dr. Donnelly has a gentle manner, but it really doesn't soften the news he delivers.

"The CT scan showed a large mass in Annie's abdomen and another smaller one by her uterus," Dr. Donnelly says. "It could be a cyst, but the radiologist described it as a large loculated complex 14 cm mass that is worrisome for neoplastic disease, which simply means new growth or tumor."

Mom and I are stunned silent. We believe we have just heard Annie's death sentence. Dr. Donnelly sits down on the foot of Annie's bed and continues to talk about what the possible next steps are.

"The next logical step would be to do a biopsy," he says.

Mom immediately discounts it. "We do not want to put Annie through anything that is going to cause her to suffer more," she says.

"The other thing we could do is biopsy the growth by Annie's uterus," Dr. Donnelly says. "It is a less-invasive procedure than would be required to biopsy the larger growth near her stomach, but it might definitively tell us if the growth is cancerous."

I am going over the possible scenarios in my mind. If they biopsy the tumor and it is malignant, what are our choices? Surgery? Chemotherapy? Neither of those choices sounds feasible to me. Do we really have an option of making Annie better without surgery? Probably not.

"We do not want to put her through anything else," my mom says.

"The radiologist believes by the look of the mass that it is likely cancer, but he can't be conclusive without the biopsy," Dr. Donnelly says.

We are not going to let anyone cut on Annie. We're done. We want to take her home. We express this desire, and Dr. Donnelly says he will ask the nurses to contact Hospice. We can leave whenever we are ready today.

Dr. Donnelly stands up and starts to walk out of the room. I ask, "What would you do if it were your child?"

He stops and is silent for a moment while he thinks over his answer. "Probably exactly what you are doing," he says, and then he leaves.

Mom and I are both in tears. Mom stands up. She is trying to say something but the words seem choppy, as if she is having difficulty expelling them from her mouth. They come out one forced syllable at a time. She says, "I ... al ... ways ... prayed ... I'd ... out ... live ... her."

It is almost unbearable to look at Annie's smiling face.

Right at that moment, the hematologist saunters into the room looking down at Annie's chart in his hands. "I have good news," he says. He looks up from Annie's chart and notices we are crying. "Is something wrong?" he asks.

"We just got some bad news that Annie probably has cancer," I say. "She is going home today."

The hematologist utters, "I'm sorry," and quietly starts to back out of the room. "Do you want to tell us your news?" I ask. "The blood levels have responded very well to the transfusions," he says. We thank him, and then he leaves.

I look at Annie and say, "You get to go home now, Sweetheart." We have been avoiding the "home" word until now because we didn't want to get her excited and get her hopes up. "We're getting out of this place," I say.

I go into the hall to call Carol and tell her the news. I know my dad will be coming soon, and I know he will take this news very hard. Mom and I talk it over and ask a nurse if there is a private conference room that my parents can use. The nursing staff is very accommodating, and they place a privacy sign on the door of a sitting room down the hall. Carol plans to drop Dad off at the hospital entrance, so he won't have to walk from the parking garage. She calls me and lets me know when they are on their way. I travel down the elevator and through the long hallways to meet him at the lobby door.

I feel like I am leading a lamb to the slaughter. He wants to know what the CT scan results are. I say, "Mom will tell you all about it." I take him to the conference room where Mom is waiting, and I return to Annie's room to wait with Carol.

Although we knew Annie was very sick, although we hated to see her suffer, although I believed it would be a miracle if she recovered, knowing is different. Knowing is final. Knowing is devoid of any hope. Knowing creates a prickling heightened sense of awareness in me. Everything we say, everything we do, acquires a heavy significance and becomes indelibly printed on my mind. The little microcosm of life and the scene we're in becomes sharply clear while the surrounding atmosphere blurs into a foggy gray.

The very worst part of knowing that Annie is going to die is knowing that Annie won't know, and there is no way we can tell her. She thinks she is going home and she is happy.

After a period of time my mom and dad come back into the room. My dad is openly crying. He says, "My girl's finally going to get her wings."

Once we decide to go, things happen rapidly. Hospice nurses arrive almost immediately. They speak with Annie's nurse out in the hall and buzz about making phone calls to set up what will be needed at home. They are happy to hear that Annie already has a hospital bed; that will make things easier. Meanwhile Annie's nurse starts removing the things from her that were so essential just yesterday. She disconnects the monitors and carefully removes the stickers from Annie's chest. She disconnects the IV that now enters through Annie's picc line. Then she quickly removes the picc line by grasping it and pulling it out. Annie is startled, but doesn't seem to be in pain.

We will be administering Annie's pain medicines at home. A hospice nurse will visit us tonight to make sure we understand how everything will work. I go into the hall where the hospice nurse is working, and I ask her if they will be able to give us a warning when they think Annie's passing is imminent. She tells me they can usually tell when things start to move in that direction, but not always. Mark and I have a five-day trip scheduled to Maine and are planning to leave on Saturday. I am trying to decide if I should cancel it. "How much time do you think she has?" I ask. I don't know whether we are looking at months, weeks, or days.

"Typically an individual will not last past two weeks after having stopped eating," the hospice nurse says. This confuses me a little bit because technically Annie hasn't eaten much for probably close to two weeks already, but she got the IV fluids and the blood transfusions, so I don't know what it all means in terms of time. I've been worrying out loud about whether I should go or cancel the trip. There is a no-refund policy at the bed and breakfast we have reservations at in Maine. If Annie survives two weeks, I could still be back home to spend the last week with her and my family. My mom and dad tell me I should go. Although I have lost my enthusiasm for the trip, I fear that canceling the trip and staying will add a heightened sense of doom to the situation. I still have a couple of days before I leave. I will decide later.

The ambulance comes to take Annie home at about 6:00 p.m. Carol and I collect all of Annie's, Mom's and our own personal belongings that have accumulated in the room and leave.

Hospice DNR, or "do not resuscitate," comfort care protocol is activated immediately. The hospice nurse at the hospital tells Mom to place DNR signs in Annie's room in case emergency personnel are summoned. Right when she gets home, Mom finds a wide red magic marker and scrawls DNR in big capital letters across three papers. She tapes all three in Annie's room using torn pieces of masking tape. They hang crooked on her dresser and two of her walls. She does this resolutely; it is something that needs to be done. Annie is in such bad shape Mom doesn't want to prolong anything that is going to happen. Mom has silenced her heart and is functioning out of necessity, not thinking about the fact that the words are proclaiming, "Allow her to die."

We are uneasy about, and even intimidated by, now administering Annie's heavy-duty pain medicine without the help of professionals. The oxycodone comes as a liquid in a small vial with a syringe. Annie is supposed to get 0.25 ml every four hours.

At about 9:00 p.m. it is getting close to the time to give Annie another dose of her pain medicine. Mom, Carol and I stand in the kitchen as Mom opens the vial and tries to measure this miniscule quantity of liquid. We are confused because the syringe bottom narrows to a flat tip that extends lower than the circular seal the syringe makes with the wall of the vial. We aren't sure whether we should measure from the tip of the syringe, or from the seal. We are afraid we might give Annie an overdose, but we also want to make sure she is getting enough medicine to stop the pain. The tension in the kitchen heightens as Mom, Carol and I all take a turn examining the syringe.

When we left the hospital over three hours ago, we were informed that a nurse would visit us tonight to answer any questions and help us get started at home. At 9:30 p.m. I call the hospice help line and ask when we might expect this nurse.

I tell the nurse who answers the phone that we don't understand the directions on how to draw up and administer the Oxycodone and we're worried that Annie is in pain. She talks me through the correct use of the syringe and the measurement of the correct amount of liquid. She instructs me to place the medication under Annie's tongue. I relay the directions to Mom who will be administering Annie's medicine every four hours. She will have to get up at 2:00 a.m. and 6:00 a.m. to give Annie her pain medicine through the night. Right now she is unwilling to delegate this responsibility to anybody else.

The nurse finally visits after midnight and confirms that we used the Oxycodone syringe correctly. She also tells us that although Annie's dose is 0.25 ml, we can give her up to 0.5 ml if she needs it for the pain. She says this is a very small dose and will likely increase over time, so we shouldn't be overly worried about an overdose.

Tonight I am extremely angry that Annie has to go through this after the life she has had to lead. I don't know why she *couldn't* have died peacefully and quietly in her chair in front of the television where she used to nap occasionally. I don't understand why she is going to have to suffer what can only be a painful, frightening and prolonged death. I don't understand why her. She can't even tell us if she's hurting so we have to guess by facial expressions. We know when it gets bad because she starts blowing her cheeks out or puffing. But we don't know if the pain ever goes away, and in this world of hospice, you have ranges of medication that you can give to control the pain. But how do you really know with Annie if you *are* controlling the pain?

This is going to be hard to bear.

I start praying that she is released from any suffering very soon. I e-mail my friends and ask them to pray for Annie and for my parents.

2006

When I interviewed my parents for the class I was taking I wanted to know what their concerns were about Annie's care. I wanted to know if they would do anything different. I wanted to know if they feared for the future. I wondered if they considered having Annie re-evaluated with modern testing methods.

"I know you don't want to put her through this, but a CT scan could possibly give you a lot of information that you don't have," I said.

"Well, we've thought about the CT scan," Mom said.

"What's the point?" Dad asked.

"Well, it would ease your mind, or just for curiosity," I answered.

"That's the point. I won't put her through that for curiosity's sake," Dad said.

"You have to hold your head still. She wouldn't like that," Mom explained.

"Well, there may be no point in it, but you might find out that actually she's got more brain than you thought; it just developed somewhere different," I argued.

"Oh I know she's got more brain than we thought," Mom said. "The first place, the front portion of the brain is the emotional part. I mean let's face it. She's got plenty of emotions. She doesn't cry, but if she gets hurt bad enough she would. She was biting her finger one time when she was a little kid; she started crying."

I continued on with my questions. "What concerns you the most about taking care of Annie?" I asked.

"Being able to interpret what her needs are," Dad immediately responded.

"If she gets something, like a cold, then I get concerned because things happen, and there's no way she can tell me, and I just have to guess," Mom said.

"One of the worst things that can happen around here is to put Diane to bed and have her cough," Dad said with a twinkle in his eye. "That's a no-sleep night."

Mom and I both laughed and then Mom tried to defend herself. "Well, I can explain that," she said. "If you don't get her stopped, she gets to coughing and strangling, and that's a very scary thing to go through. Then I believe she gets asthma. I don't know for sure, but it seems like she's got something going on. So at all costs, I try to stop her coughing at the very beginning so she doesn't continue it. She gets scared when that happens. And when she gets scared then everything else gets bad, too."

"Do you have any regrets?" I asked next. "What is your biggest regret?"

"My biggest regret," Mom said and stopped to think for a minute. "I don't really have any regret. I get frustrated. I got frustrated a lot more when she was younger than I do now because I was also trying to deal with you and your sister. You know what I usually tell people when they ask me that, or say 'I couldn't do that'? I say, 'Oh yes you could. Yes you could. You were never faced with it.' I'd be willing to bet most of the people I've talked to would have done the same thing."

Dad said, "All I know is that very early on we were both quite young and had no idea what was down the line. We made a decision. She's the way God gave her to us, and we agreed to take on that responsibility. There was no pressure from anybody else to do it or not do it. We chose to do it." After a moment he added, "She's been a major pleasure to me on a one-to-one basis."

"And she has been a major pleasure to a lot of other people, some of whom do not even know her," Mom said. "I think it's because she just smiles. She has some kind of charisma there that doesn't have to be spoken. She'll look up at people and just smile. And they'll melt right there. They don't remember our names, but they'll remember her name.

"You can take her to the store; you can take her anywhere, and the way she's sitting back, she can see people's faces good. And she'll just look up and smile, and you've got everybody in the place smiling at her. But I think any ordinary person could do that too, I just don't think we do.

"She is no threat to anybody. It's not like if you love her, she's going to do something to hurt you. She's not going to ever do anything that's going to make us unhappy."

I had been talking to my parents for over two hours and was down to my last question. "Does the future worry you?" I asked.

"We've got the beginning of a plan," Mom said mentioning the fact that at this point, although they weren't using DDS services, Annie was signed up for them.

"It worries Dad," Mom continued. "I don't think about it much. And that's probably a head-in-the-sand type of thing. But Dad talks about it. He's concerned about it. I feel like, so far we've handled everything as it's come along, so I think that everything will turn out for the best. And that's really leaving it up to somebody else, not necessarily you kids. I believe that's leaving what's going to happen up to God."

100

2003 | *I am on the left beside Dad, and Mom. Carol holds Annie's hand to keep it from blocking her face.*

CHAPTER 15 **Saying Goodbye**

Day 14

Thursday August 6

Annie's medication is turning into a point of contention. This morning I go into Annie's room, and Mom and Dad are in there. Mom has given Annie her 0.25 ml of medicine, but I think Annie still looks like she's in pain. Mom doesn't want to give her anymore. I argue with her and tell her if it were me, I would want to have as much medicine as I was allowed to have. I don't understand Mom's reluctance to give Annie a larger dose. I'm also worried Mom is going to continue to try to get Annie to eat. I worry that my parents are still concerned about building up Annie's strength. I'm afraid they don't really understand that Annie isn't going to get stronger. She's not going to get better. I ask Mom not to ask Annie to try to eat. Annie has not been able to keep food down. People, particularly cancer patients, will naturally stop eating as they progress towards death. I believe Annie might try to please Mom by eating, even though she doesn't want to. Mom says, "But Annie might be hungry."

Mom turns to Dad who is slouching in the pink recliner beside Annie's bed. "What do you think, Jerry?" she asks. "Do you think she is still in pain?" Dad just sits silently. He seems to have lost all sense of what to do.

Mom is trying to follow directions. "I'll give her the 0.25 ml and if she still looks like she's in pain in a half hour, I will give her more." I get a piece of notebook paper so Mom can chart all of the medicines she is responsible for giving to Annie. The responsibility of determining how much medicine Annie needs, and then administering it, may be more stressful for Mom than trying to get Annie to drink was before they took her to the hospital. And I'm not sure how my mom is going to be able to administer Annie's pain medicine to her around the clock, getting up twice a night.

Today is a day of tying up loose ends before I leave to go home to Cincinnati and possibly to Maine on Saturday. I spend the morning taking my dad on errands— to the bank, Best Buy, and then to lunch. Dad wants new headphones for his iPod and a dock or speaker system for it. Since his iPod is truly the only thing that brings him consolation right now, and he really does seem peaceful when he uses it, I take him to Best Buy for the speakers. Also, my parents' answering machine died today. They have been getting a lot of calls from friends and family because of Annie's condition, and it is not always convenient to answer the phone.

Dad and I do not make very fast progress, largely because he has trouble walking. When we finish at the bank and Best Buy, I drop him back at home and go to the grocery store alone.

In the afternoon between setting up the phone, and teaching Dad how to use the iPod speakers, I telephone our DDS caseworker Rob to discuss a schedule for our home health care aide Christiana that doesn't conflict with the Hospice schedule. Then I call Hospice. A skilled nurse has visited us today, and a meeting is scheduled with Annie's caseworker Janice for tomorrow morning.

Annie is resting peacefully and sleeping on and off in her room. Mark has come to have dinner with us and then take me home.

When it is time to leave, I tiptoe back to Annie's room and peek in the door to see if she is still asleep. I want to say goodbye to her before I leave, but I don't want to wake her up. At first I am disappointed because I think she is asleep, but then she stirs and opens her eyes as if she senses I am there.

I walk to her side and lean over the railing, allowing my hair to fall on her right hand that she holds up close to her face, like usual. For once, I do not take her hand and hold it to try to protect my hair from her grasp. I'm going to let her have it if she wants it. And she does run her fingers in my hair, but never quite grabs hold. She's very gentle as she crosses her fingers over a strand of my hair. I don't know if she is too weak or if she just wants to touch it and has learned how.

I gently press my forehead to hers and speak in a whisper. Annie is looking straight in my eyes, her eyes big and a soft brown blur through my own. "I love you, Sweetheart. Everybody loves you," I say.

"No worries.

"Don't wait for me. You go when you're ready.

"Everybody is going to be okay. We're all going to be okay.

"I'm going to take care of Mom and Dad. You don't have to worry.

"I'm so happy for you.

"I'm so happy you are my sister.

"I'll be looking for you. Everywhere.

"You'd better be looking for me.

"I'll see you again.

"No worries."

Annie smiles at times and starts making soft vocal noises like she is talking to me, and I encourage her. "Yes. Yes," I say.

"I hear you.

"I know you love me too.

"I know you love everybody. I will tell them for you.

"Goodbye little sister.

"I'll be back. But don't wait for me. You go when you're ready.

"No worries."

1960s–present

Although Annie was happy and smiled a lot, she responded to various situations with a variety of facial expressions that prompted the rest of us to speak for her. She might roll her eyes away from over-the-top silliness as if to say, "Will you guys *please* grow up." Or if she got a hold of something, like your hair, she'd get a determined look on her face as if she thought, There's no way I'm giving this up without a fight. When she was eating sometimes she would clamp her teeth together as if to say, "I'm done. I refuse to open my mouth and good luck making me." Often we would speak for her and say something like, "Annie says, 'It's hot and sticky out here and the sun is in my eyes. Will someone *please* take me inside?'"

In this way Annie did participate in conversations, family gatherings, or just day-to-day life. During an energized discussion over the dinner table, I might turn to Annie who sat near-by and ask, "What do you think of all of this, Annie?" And she would generally acknowledge my question with a smile and turn of her head. Dad might call out from the far end of the table, "Girl! Where's my pretty girl?"

Although she smiled a lot, Annie also exhibited other emotions that we did our best to interpret and acknowledge. Sometime after I had moved out on my own, Dad had the opportunity to visit a friend in Wisconsin and go hunting for a week. It was the only time I can remember him going away on his own. When he got back after being gone for seven days, Annie wouldn't look at him. I guess she was mad that he left her, and she gave him the cold shoulder for a while.

Annie was a great listener. She listened for sounds in the house like a garage door opening or a voice from the next room. When she was hungry, if she heard the 'pop' sound from opening the lid of a baby food jar my mom was preparing for her dinner, Annie got excited. I could be in the family room with her watching TV and all of a sudden she would get excited. I would wonder why and then as a delayed reaction, I would hear Mom working in the kitchen. "Are you getting hungry, Sweetheart?" I'd ask. "You hear Mom making your dinner, don't you?"

Annie was also great at just listening to us—no questions, no advice, no disapproval—she simply listened. When I baby-sat for her in high school, we had girl-to-girl talks. I leaned my arms on the wooden chair dad made and talked to her, pouring out all of my teenage angst. I knew I could tell her anything and she wouldn't repeat a word of it. Sometimes I rested my forearms on the arm of her chair, laid my head on my arms and talked and cried to her to my heart's content. And even though mostly she laughed or hollered when I talked to her, on these occasions she somehow knew it was a serious matter. Annie was a great listener. She saw and heard a lot of what went on in that house.

Mom always said, "If Annie ever talks, we're all going to be in trouble."

2000 | *Annie communicates with her facial expressions and body language.*

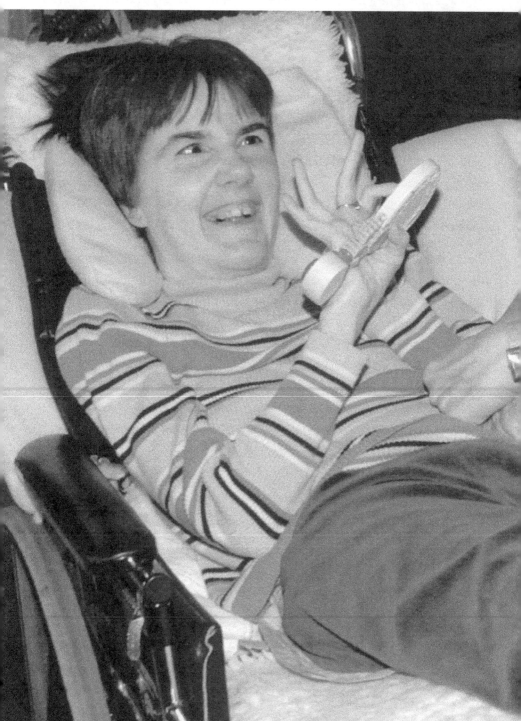

CHAPTER 16 **What to Expect**

Day 15
Friday August 7

I plan to stay in phone contact with my mom and Carol today. They are busy with hospice activities. The skilled nurse came and took Annie's vital signs. Then she spent time with my parents, providing education on pain management, nutrition and hydration, and oxygen use, although the oxygen has not been delivered yet. We are all concerned that Annie's death is imminent, and we do not know what to look for or what to expect. The nurse provided a book about what to expect when someone is dying and discussed the contents with my mom. When asked if she would like both the social worker and chaplain to visit, Mom said yes.

I have decided to go to Maine tomorrow. Mark has reassured me we can get a flight home if we need to return.

September 1984

"It's time for lunch, Annie," I said. "I know it's been a long time since I've fed you, but it's going to be okay. You're going to eat like a good girl."

I was twenty-seven years old, married, and with two small children of my own. I was babysitting Annie for a few days so that my parents could go on a trip. From the beginning, my parents taught us how to look out for Annie, making sure she wasn't left alone in a room, or wasn't having a seizure, or wasn't falling out of her chair.

Annie doesn't really have a lot of seizures anymore like she used to when she was little. I knew she was having a seizure if her face got pale, her mouth started twitching, and her whole body tensed up. I could see fear, even terror, in her eyes. It seemed as if she were trapped inside a foreign, mechanical body and couldn't get out. If I saw that happen, I knew what to do.

"Mom! Annie's having a seizure!" I immediately yelled.

And Mom would drop whatever she was doing and come running. But Annie's seizures were usually very short, and there wasn't anything Mom could really do about them except wait for them to pass. I suppose she was always on guard in case it turned into a grand mal seizure and she would need to seek emergency medical help. But that only happened once.

Annie had a grand mal seizure when she was real little. My dad rushed her to the hospital and ran for help through the hall, with her in his arms stiff and not breathing. After that, Annie was put on two seizure medicines, Phenobarbital and Dilantin, which kept the seizures under control for the most part.

As she grew older Annie still had small seizures where she stared off into space for a moment, but you could call her back from those.

"Annie, where are you?"

Or you could move your hand in front of her eyes to break the stare. She'd blink her eyes and return to the present.

As we grew older Mom and Dad taught us how to take care of Annie's physical needs—how to feed her, dress her and put her to bed at night. But although they taught us how to take care of Annie, my parents made a conscious effort not to burden us with her care. They never placed expectations on us regarding her care at the present or for the future.

It had been probably at least five, and maybe ten, years since I'd fed Annie. Right after I graduated from college in 1979, I moved to Cincinnati for a job. For the four years before that, I was in college and not living at home. So although I used to feed Annie quite regularly when I babysat for her while I was in high school, it had been several years, and I was a little bit nervous. I knew that Annie could get excited, or laugh, or cough and any of that could turn into a choking or breathing issue if you were feeding her. I never worried about it when I was younger because I was used to feeding her, and she was used to me. But now my visits were something of a novelty for her, and she always got excited when I was around and paying any attention to her.

I was preparing her for the meal by trying to talk to her in a matter-of-fact and no-nonsense way to keep her calm.

"You're going to eat your lunch for me like a good girl," I repeated, as I moved about the kitchen preparing her medicine and warming her baby food in the microwave.

I pushed Annie in her chair up beside the kitchen table, with her head close to the table and her feet extending into the room. She was reclining in her chair, smiling, and watching me in that out-of-the-corner-of-her-eye way that she had of darting her eyes towards me and then away. She knew this was unusual for me to be in the kitchen making her meal and she reacted like she thought it was a game.

"I know what I'm doing," I said, reassuring myself more than her. "Here's the Phenobarbital." I took the medicine off the shelf in the cabinet and measured out ½ teaspoon into a small plastic children's drinking cup. "Okay. Now I need two teaspoons of Benadryl." I added a little bit of milk to dilute the two medicines and continued the ongoing narration like a Julia Child's television cooking demonstration. Annie just sat and listened, smiling and occasionally chuckling if my speech got too animated. Her right hand held her toy mirror up near her face as she flexed her wrist.

I gathered everything together—her medicine, a small sipper cup of milk, her warmed baby food, spoon and a terry cloth towel that I tucked under her chin and around her neck after I sat down beside her.

"You've got to put your arm down, Sweetheart," I said as I gently pressed the back of my right arm against hers, lowering it away from her face and down to her side. I carefully rested the cup of medicine against her bottom lip and tipped it into her open mouth, giving her just a small amount of liquid at a time to swallow. If I gave her too much she would choke and spit all of it back out. Even so, a little bit of the medicine did escape her mouth and began to run down her chin. I scooped it back up with the cup and continued in this fashion until the medicine was all gone.

I gave her a little drink of milk to wash down the strong bitter taste of the medicine and started in on the food. I used a spoon to feed Annie her baby food, but since her mouth did not close around it, I had to scrape the food off the spoon and into her mouth with her two front teeth. If she wouldn't open her mouth for me, I gently pressed down on her chin using my left hand. "Open up," I said as I pressed on her chin, scraped the food off, scooped what escaped off her chin with the spoon, and started all over. I continued to use the back of my arm as defense against Annie's efforts to raise her right hand to her mouth.

I started to relax. Like bicycle riding and so many other things in life, it was all coming back to me now, the rhythm and flow of feeding Annie.

I remained serious and didn't laugh or make loud or sudden movements. When she started to gag, I tried to talk her out of it. "No, you don't," I said, "you're alright. You need to swallow your food." She struggled with it for a few seconds as I held the edge of the towel in a ready position in case she decided to cough. She calmed down and we kept going.

I accidentally bumped a sensitive place in her mouth with the spoon and she flinched. This in turn made her laugh. I grabbed the bottom portion of the towel and covered her mouth with it so she wouldn't spray baby food all over me.

"I'm sorry, Sweetheart," I said. "It's okay now and you've got to eat like a good girl. We're almost done."

She calmed down and I got back to business.

I would feed her another meal later today and then three meals tomorrow and on every subsequent day until my parents returned.

Now that I had children of my own, it felt like a huge responsibility to take care of Annie. As I sat and fed Annie, I was overcome with the weight of the commitment my parents had made in taking care of my sister. Mostly I felt stunned when I realized the day-in, day-out, three-meals-a-day, no-days-off, commitment my parents had made in caring for Annie.

Over the years, when I was young and even as an adult, I struggled with disappointments of things I couldn't do, or my family couldn't do, or my parents couldn't do for me or for their grandchildren because of Annie.

When we were younger there were simply places we couldn't go as a family, limitations on what we could do as individuals needing transportation, and activities I participated in that my parents couldn't attend. Later with my own children, we could never visit if anybody was even thinking about getting sick.

A few years after my daughter Anna was born, and when her two older brothers were still quite young, Anna came down with chickenpox a couple of nights before Christmas. Mark's family was fine with us participating in their Christmas celebration because they all had had chickenpox before. But we weren't able to visit my parents. Although Annie had a mild case of chickenpox as a child when Carol and I did, Mom was always worried about anyone visiting who had a cold or virus for fear it might make Annie sick. I think with Chickenpox in particular, she was worried that Annie might get Shingles.

When Anna recovered, her two brothers broke out with the red spots. I think we finally were able to exchange presents with my parents and Annie at the end of January, long after the trees were down and the tinsel had all been swept away.

I realize this may seem small in the whole scheme of things, and my disappointment usually did make me feel like a small and petty person, but regardless, my disappointment was real. It was what I felt. It wasn't what I decided to feel, or what I thought I should feel. It was simply what I felt. In my standard modus operandi, the disappointment was immediately tromped on by the guilt for feeling the disappointment. This is a song I danced to my entire life: disappointment in my wants not being satisfied because Annie's needs must be recognized, followed by guilt at the audacity to even desire anything more at all when faced with how little my sister Annie had.

At some point while taking care of Annie this time, my eyes were opened and I witnessed in a very real way my parents' love for and commitment to her. And a new light shone on it for me. I suddenly realized that I was their daughter too, and if it had been me instead of Annie in that chair, they would be taking care of me like they were taking care of her. Such was their love for their children, and I was one of them. It was a turning point for me because

I suddenly saw all the love and devotion they poured on my sister as being directed at me too. They would have done it for me.

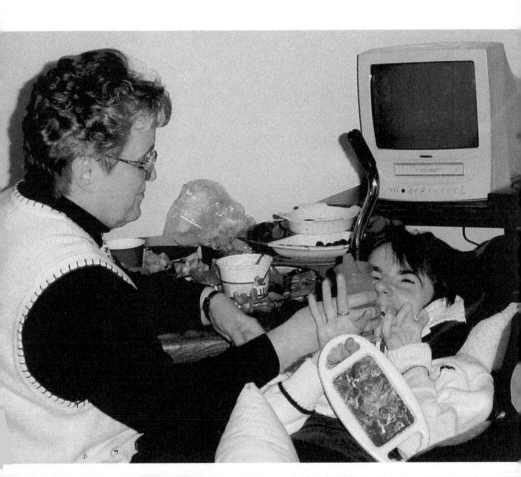

1980s | Mom feeds Annie lunch in the office at my dad's tool and die shop.

CHAPTER 17 **Flying Away**

Day 16

Saturday August 8

The plane that will carry Mark and me to Maine ascends into the air and I can feel my spirits rise as I shed the weight of my emotional burden like the ground that falls below us. The physical distance from the drama that is playing out at my parents' home brings a welcome emotional distance as well. The further we travel from Dayton and the house of sorrow, the more dissociated I become from the previous days of dread and their series of dashed hopes.

Mark and I rent a car when we arrive in Boston, and as we drive up the coast to Camden, we pass through a very dark tunnel where up ahead the light at the end looks like a beacon of hope. I think it is a good omen.

The Inn at Sunrise Point, where we have reservations, bills itself as a luxury ocean-front hideaway near Camden, Maine. All the rooms and cottages have spectacular sunrise views. Gourmet breakfasts are served each day in the conservatory.

Our room is on the second floor and is comfortable with a queen bed, two wicker chairs, a wood-burning fireplace, and a private deck with a panoramic ocean view.

On the first floor of the Inn, an expansive white porch with wooden rockers looks out over the green lawn, dotted by white Adirondack chairs, above the rocky shore. The ocean sparkles in the distance where it spreads to meet the horizon.

Mark and I take a walk across the lawn and down the wooden steps to a small rocky beach where individuals have built miniature monuments, piles really, of stones.

Later we sit on our deck overlooking the water. I feel a little guilty and undeserving that I am here in such a beautiful place while my family remains at home struggling with Annie's pain and decline.

Seagulls glide across the sky as if they haven't a care in the world. They make me think of my great Aunt Agnes for some unknown reason, and I add her to the list of deceased relatives who might aid Annie on her journey if such is possible. Since Aunt Agnes devoted her life to God and the Catholic Church as a Sister of Mercy, I feel she might have some sway in the afterlife. I can't believe I have forgotten to ask her for help before now.

Throughout Annie's illness I have been beseeching my deceased relatives for their intercession—my grandmother, my grandfather, my aunt Nancy and Uncle Mike who both recently died, and my extremely faith-filled father-in-law who died a little over a year ago. I am keeping almost a direct line open to prayer. When I am not distracted by something in the present moment, I am aware of the prayer to Mary the Mother of Jesus, the Memorarae, constantly playing through my mind on an automatically restarting loop.

> *Remember O most gracious Virgin Mary*
> *Never was it known*
> *That anyone who fled to thy protection*
> *Implored thy help*
> *Or sought thy intercession*
> *Was left unaided.*
> *Inspired by this confidence I fly unto thee*
> *O virgin of virgins my mother*
> *To thee do I come*

Before thee I stand
Sinful and sorrowful
O Mother of the Word Incarnate
Despise not my petitions,
But in thy mercy
Hear and answer me

We drive into Camden to a small restaurant that has been recommended by the folks at the Inn. It is in a house nestled in the woods that has been converted to a restaurant. The interior is charming, and is decorated with original pieces of artwork that are for sale. The food is homemade and delicious; they are famous for their desserts.

It is dark when we return to the Inn but we leave the curtains and our sliding glass doors to the deck open so we can see and hear the ocean. From our bed we can see moonlight shining down on the water and streaking to the shore like a beacon from a lighthouse.

Both the seagulls earlier in the day, and now the moonlight across the water, bring me a sense of peace and comfort.

"I'm glad we decided to come," I tell Mark. My soul is being fed.

2008

After an episode where Dad was hospitalized for heart trouble a couple of years ago, I got concerned that we might be in big trouble if something happened to Mom and she wasn't able to communicate with us about Annie's care. Neither Carol or I knew all the specific details of how they took care of her anymore. I brought my computer with me to visit my parents and sat with my mom in the dining room one day, generating a document that detailed Annie's care:

ANNIE'S CARE DOCUMENT

Annie wakes up in the morning between 7:00 and 8:00. We turn her over on her back, raise the head of her bed, and cover her back up. We put music on, either her radio or her CDs. Around 9:00, sometimes later, we get her up. First we change her diaper (every time we change her diaper throughout the day we wipe her off with the wet wipe.) A pad goes in the center of the diaper. More diapers are in the closet. A lidded garbage can is in her closet for the used diapers. She can spend the day in her pajamas. We put on little slippers or pull on socks for daywear.

Then we put her in her chair, making sure she has her neck pillow on. She sits on the lambs' wool that should already be on the chair.

Breakfast

Annie has breakfast right away. Towels for around her neck are located in the pantry.

First she gets her medicine:

> Phenobarbital Liquid – ½ tsp
>
> Dilantin – ½ tsp
>
> Cough Syrup (Generic for Rhondec DM Syrup RF) – 1 tsp

The liquid meds are mixed with a little warm milk and given to her with a medicine dropper, a little at a time. If you put it in the back of her mouth she is more likely to swallow it.

She eats the following for breakfast:

> 1 jar of strained baby food cereal (mixed, rice or oatmeal, with a little sugar added and heated in microwave for 50 sec. on 30% power until it is lukewarm, like you would test for a baby's food)

1 glass of warm apple juice (5 oz. sipper cup heated 1 min. in microwave at 30%)

We brush Annie's teeth after breakfast with a toothbrush that is located in the cabinet by her medicines, dipped in a mixture of lemon juice, water and artificial sweetener. She doesn't really like it, but if you do it gently, you can get it done. Stop if she starts gagging.

Most of the time we take her into the family room after breakfast and turn on the TV to either the Disney channel or the cartoon channel. If we are going to be in the kitchen, sometimes she just stays in there with us. Usually if she goes into the family room, she takes a little nap in her chair.

Lunch

Annie eats better if there is a five-hour time period between meals. For lunch:

Phenobarbital – ½ teaspoon

Benadryl – 2 teaspoons

1 container of yogurt (Yoplait original yogurt (6 oz), smooth, no lumps, no whole fruit (French Vanilla, Key Lime, Orange, Strawberry if fruit can be picked out))

1 cup of lukewarm milk in a sipper cup

If someone is working in the kitchen, Annie stays in the kitchen for a little while.

Afternoon Rest

About 3:30 or 4:00 we put her in her bed and change her diaper. Doing this while the bed is flat is easier. Then we raise the head of her bed to an angle about ½ of that used on her chair. Annie needs to have her neck pillow behind her head. Again, we turn on the radio or CD for her to listen to. Her radio stays on station 99.1 or 99.9 (Country music channels) all the time. She rests about two or three hours, although she doesn't sleep. About 6:00 (or four hours after her last Benadryl) we give her the Benadryl while she is in her bed. Just roll the bed up a little higher and use the medicine dropper.

Dinner

We usually get Annie back up around 6:30 or 7:00 and feed her dinner:

> No medicine at dinner
>
> Cereal (like at breakfast)
>
> 1 cup of lukewarm milk
>
> Pudding (4 oz. at room temperature, any kind except chocolate)

After dinner she stays in the kitchen with us until it is cleaned up, and then we usually all go into the family room together.

Bedtime

Bedtime is between 9:30 and 10:00. We give her bedtime medicine:

> Phenobarbital – 1 teaspoon
>
> Dilantin – ½ teaspoon
>
> Benadryl – (about 4 hours after last dose) 2 teaspoons, with a small amount (2 or 3 oz.) of lukewarm and de-carbonated 7-Up or Sprite

We put Annie in bed on her back, being sure that the bed is flat; change her diaper; change her clothes, and take off her socks. Then we roll her onto her stomach. After she is turned over, her left hand has to be checked to make sure it is not twisted. She sleeps with it under her, but it needs to be flat. We pick up her left shoulder and make sure her pillow gets between her shoulder and her left hand. The left elbow needs to be tucked up to her side and not sticking out or up, so that she can lay her head down. Her legs need to be straightened out. They can be criss-crossed but the right leg has to be free to move, or over the top of the left one.

We rub her back and brush her hair every night. Often we put a half-full hot water bottle on her lower back at night to help her relax. She does not sleep with a nightlight, but we do have a device that creates "Nature's Soothing Sounds" that drowns out noises. We have it tuned in on rain.

Miscellaneous

Other medications Annie takes as needed:

> Tylenol suppositories (325 mg – ½ of suppository (located in door of refrigerator))

> Nasal spray (regular neosynephrine – is used if she has a cold or cough)

> Cough syrup (cannot be given at the same time as the Benadryl, but can be used at night instead of the Benadryl if she has a cough)

> Phenegren suppositories for nausea (located in door of refrigerator, she gets ½ of suppository)

Annie wears Attends diapers with a doubler pad. They are delivered to the house on a schedule and paid for by credit card. Phone # is 1-800-538-1036.

We give Annie a sponge bath about once a week. She gets scared when she has all of her clothes off at one time, so we wash the top half first and then the bottom half. We put an old playpen pad (located in her closet) covered with a towel on her bed, then lay her on top of that. We cover her unclothed body parts with a large bath towel while we wash her. We put a no-rinse body wash (like the astronauts use) in a basin of water on the stand beside the bed and wash her with a wet (don't wring it clear out) washrag, dry her off, and put lotion all over her body. Her hair gets washed separately at another time.

We use no-rinse shampoo. We protect the bed with the disposable blue hospital pads. Lay Annie flat on the bed. Squirt the shampoo on her hair, being careful not to get it in her eyes. Massage it in until all the hair is wet. Follow the bottle directions. The foaming provides the rinsing action. Dry her hair with a towel and comb. We would do this in the afternoon when we lay her down. We shampoo her hair every couple of weeks or more often if needed.

Annie receives a Social Security disability check monthly and is on Medicare with a supplemental insurance policy paid by the state called QMB.

We own a life insurance policy on Annie with Prudential. It is paid quarterly.

Annie usually goes for a medical check-up once a year.

Annie has been deemed eligible for Montgomery County Board of Developmental Disabilities services.

Annie is allergic to trees and pollen, etc. That is why she takes the Benadryl. We always use the air-conditioner and do not open the windows to the outdoors.

I saved this document on my computer and printed out a couple of copies for Mom. She put one in an envelope that she decorated with a border of lace and taped to the wall in Annie's bedroom.

circa 1972 | *Mom helps Dad hold Annie for her annual Easter portrait. Annie still has her eye glasses.*

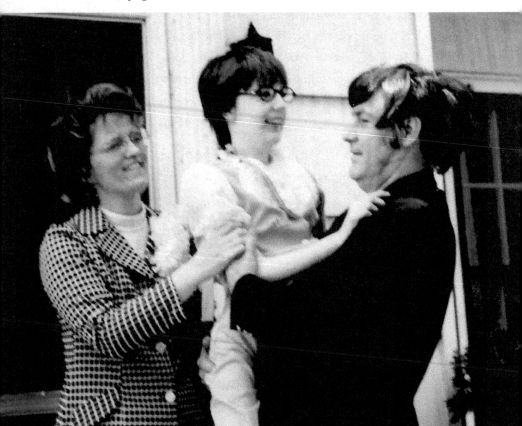

CHAPTER 18 **Crisis Mode**

Day 17
Sunday August 9

This little cocoon of peace and surrealism I've built from distance, the calming nature of the ocean shore, and this peaceful bed and breakfast lasts only until I call Carol after breakfast. In my last conversation with her before I left, Carol asked me if I wanted to know over the phone if Annie dies while I am gone. I told her not to tell me until I get home. I do not want to ride on an airplane with that knowledge. Carol said, "Well, don't call and ask me how she is, then. I won't be able to lie about it."

I tell her I have changed my mind about that this morning. I need to know what is going on. "Was it because of what I said about not calling?" she asks.

"Partly," I answer.

"Annie went into crisis mode last night," Carol says. "She is on oxygen now."

"What happened?"

"I don't know. Mom and I were trying to turn her over to her back from her stomach so Mom could give her medicine, and she started coughing and couldn't get her breath. Her lips turned blue. 'She needs oxygen,' I told Mom. We called the hospice number, and they came right away with oxygen."

This morning Carol called the hospice number again to tell them that the pain medicines are not holding. Although the primary RN told Mom that Annie's pain meds could be given every two hours, it is not going to be feasible for Mom, at the age of 75, to get up through the night and manage this. "Annie is on crisis care now," Carol says. "She will have nurses here around the clock."

"Do you think I need to come home? Are they telling you anything?"

"The nurse said that anyone who is coming, should come."

After I hang up with Carol, Mark calls the airlines on his cell phone. He spends the next hour trying to find a way for us to get back home. We have used frequent-flyer miles to travel, and that seems to be causing the problem. I can hear that he is getting passed from person to person over the phone. I know this because he is explaining our situation and family crisis over and over again. He is frustrated and finally tells them to just get us tickets and we will pay for them if we have to.

I feel bad because this is turning out to be a very expensive 24 hours in Maine. The bed and breakfast we are at has a no-refunds policy, and now we are going to have to pay a premium price for tickets home. Mark doesn't seem to care. He is on a mission to get me home.

Finally he is able to connect with a manager, or someone who has the authority to be a little flexible, and he manages to get us flights out of Boston very early in the morning. We are able to use our frequent-flyer miles.

While Mark is negotiating a flight for us, nervous energy carries me through my shower and as I pack my toiletries and clothes into the suitcase. I spend the rest of the time sitting in the wicker chair looking out the glass doors to the ocean beyond. A peaceful calm has descended upon me. The goal of our upcoming journey is fearsome and awful, but the path is cut clearly and there is no way out. A calm acceptance takes over. The end of this drama with Annie is near. I am grateful that it is happening quickly. I have already asked my friends to pray that Annie dies soon. I can't stand to see her in pain and suffering. I continue to pray with all my heart that she goes soon.

After breakfast we talk to the innkeeper and explain that we have to shorten our trip because my sister is dying. They don't say anything about the charges but simply extend their sympathy and tell us they hope we will be able to visit there again in the future. They charge us only for one night's stay.

We have a few hours before we have to make the drive to Boston. We have decided to spend the night near the airport since the flight is so early in the morning and we don't want to risk missing it because of traffic.

Mark and I walk around the small downtown area of Camden and look at the sailboats off shore and the lobster traps stacked outside of restaurants. We have a quiet lunch of lobster then return to our room, pack up, and leave for the roughly three-hour drive to Boston.

late 1960s

I found out that Annie probably wasn't going to live very long when I was about nine or ten, and we were on a camping trip in a remote area at the top of the mountains near Sparta, North Carolina. We had just eaten dinner on our campsite picnic table when Annie got sick and was struggling to breathe. We got up from the table, left all of our dirty dishes and leftover food right where they were, and piled into the station wagon for the long winding drive down the wooded mountainside. Dad drove while Mom held Annie in the front seat praying that she would keep breathing.

I don't remember much being said on the way to the hospital. But when we left Annie and Mom there and drove back to pack up our gear and move to a hotel in town near the hospital, Dad got all serious and started stuttering and talking to us in his stern lecture voice as he drove through the night. We sat as still as little statues on the back seat. Annie must have been about eight years old at the time, so maybe Dad thought that was it. Maybe he thought her time was up. He was pretty convincing to us too. We were driving back up the mountain on a now dark and winding road in silence when Dad said, "Your sister Annie is not like most people." He said, "She's probably not going to live a very long time like most people do. We can't expect her to live a long time."

I didn't say a word. I was scared. We had just raced down a mountainside to a hospital with Annie. We had just left Annie and Mom behind at that same hospital. I believed my dad in everything he said. I was afraid Annie might die that night. For the next days, weeks, and even months, long after Annie recovered, was released from the hospital and we were home again, I was afraid Annie was going to die.

When we got back to the campsite, we found the bag of ice Dad had asked the neighbor to pick up for us leaned against a tree, melting. We must have had dirty dinner dishes and pots and pans to pack up, as well as all the other camping gear. But the only thing I remember is the ice bag melting against the tree. I think the neighbor must have stopped back to inquire what had happened, and I suspect he helped my dad get the camper packed up and taken down. We drove back down the mountain in the dark.

1959 | *Annie at the time of her initial eight-year prognosis.*

CHAPTER 19

Fear of Imminence

Day 18
Monday August 10

Mark gets in the ticket line at the airport to check our luggage while I take the opportunity to use the restroom. There is a young woman standing behind him when I return. She is much thinner and a little shorter than me and has long deep brown hair. I wonder if Annie might have looked something like this had she not been disabled. As I try to pass her to rejoin Mark I say, "Excuse me."

She turns to look at me, smiles and responds, "No worries." I try to smile, but the tears fill my eyes at hearing Annie's mantra, and I look down at the ground instead.

Because we had to practically beg these airline tickets, Mark and I are not able to sit together on the flight back to Cincinnati. I am a little bit worried about this because I am afraid I may be crying the whole trip, which will be awkward if I am squeezed in between two total strangers. I grimace when I see my seat. I am smashed in the middle of two young men, both of whom look to be somewhere in their late twenties or early thirties. They're going to love it if I am sobbing the whole way home, I think.

Fortunately for me, and probably them too, I maintain my composure the whole flight except for one small tearful lapse from which I quickly recover. If they notice, they don't act like it.

Any time my mind rests for a moment, I become aware of the constant fervent prayer I am sending above, "Please help her." It's like a direct line, an umbilical cord, pulsing to a father or mother in heaven, "Help her, please. Pull her into your arms. Take her from her suffering here."

When we arrive in Cincinnati mid-morning, Mark drives me directly to Dayton. Nerves that have returned with a vengeance have harshly displaced the miraculous calm that descended on me in Maine. I am thankful Mark is with me so I don't have to drive.

I don't know what I am getting into or what to expect once I get to Dayton. I haven't talked to Carol since yesterday, when we gave her our flight information. I don't know if Annie is still with us or has died in the night. I don't know if I am going to be walking into the final hours of a deathbed scene.

I decide to call Carol.

"Things are stable here," she says. "Annie has calmed down, and the immediate crisis seems under control."

The tension and dread I am starting to feel dissolves somewhat, and I can take a deep breath.

When we get to Mom and Dad's, Mark carries my suitcase inside, fortuitously already packed for several days as a result of my brief soiree to Maine.

Immediately I can sense the shift in my parents' home when Carol answers the door and follows us into the kitchen. The fear and uncertainty about what to do have now been replaced with routine.

"How are things going now?" I ask.

"About the same," she says. "Dad is taking a nap, and Mom is in Annie's room."

I cross the dining room and living room into the hall where I am assaulted by the drone of the oxygen generator positioned outside Annie's door. It looks and sounds foreign and frightening to me and drives the reality of the situation like a wedge into my stomach. Mark follows me silently into Annie's room like a protective shadow.

Everything has changed. Three table fans positioned around the room are whirring, spinning air about the room. Annie's bed has been moved away from the far wall. The foot of the bed shoots out into the room on a diagonal from the corner to allow access to both sides of her. The soft blue sheets with puffy white clouds that I gave her last year for Christmas are on the bed. Annie is lying on her stomach and makes me think of an angel lying on clouds in the sky. The foam padding I attached to the railing so that Mom could lean on it more comfortably when she was still trying to give Annie food and drinks is gone, but the three green ribbons have been tied back on in decorative bows. Annie's nightstand has been moved from beside the head of her bed on the left to against the adjacent wall on the right, where the foot of Annie's bed was previously. Bottles of pills, syringes, clear plastic cups, wipes, green sponge mouth swabs, and a bottle of lotion have replaced the stuffed animals that used to rest there.

To the left of the doorway in front of Annie's wide, sliding, closet doors a nurse sits in the pink recliner beside a little table on which a small lamp shines. The nurse is writing in a three-ring binder she holds open in her lap, but looks up and smiles at us when we enter the room.

Clear tubing from the oxygen generator snakes across the floor and up onto Annie's bed, over her ear, and across her face to her nose. Annie is facing her right hand. My mom is sitting in a kitchen chair between the nightstand and the head of the bed. Annie lifts her head up as she hears us enter the room.

"Hi Sweetheart," I say. I am trying desperately to stay upbeat and not to cry.

My mom gets up and says, "Here, you can sit down beside her."

Annie is holding her favorite mirror toy in her right hand; she flexes her wrist in greeting, but she does not smile. Her face looks like she is confused about what is happening to her. She looks like she doesn't feel well, but she is tolerating it, like so many other things she's had to tolerate in her life with no choice. "It's going to be okay, Sweetheart," I tell her as I wrap one of my hands around hers and the toy and use the other to stroke her hair back from her face. I'm not lying to her. It's going to be okay only because she is going to die and then she won't suffer anymore. But I don't tell her that. I don't even know if she knows what death is.

The oxygen tubing is indenting the skin on her face where she has lain on it. I say something to Mom about it, and she comes over and tries to readjust it. "There isn't a lot we can do with it since she's lying on her stomach," Mom says.

My mom looks like she hasn't slept in a week, and her voice sounds defeated. I don't know which is more difficult to bear—Annie's obvious discomfort or Mom's anguished surrender.

"I'm sorry you're feeling so bad, Sweetheart," I say. Annie has laid her head back down on the mattress and is looking at me. She flexes her wrist back and forth under my hand.

The nurse, whose name is Judy, tells us it is time for Annie's pain medicine. She approaches the table beside me. I feel awkward and in the way, so I stand up and huddle beside Mark near the entrance to the room while Judy uses a syringe to measure the liquid morphine and then slowly squirt it in the space between Annie's gum and cheek. She talks to me while she is doing this and explains that Annie's mouth will absorb the medicine subcutaneously. That way she won't have to swallow it and we won't have to move her back onto her back into an elevated position to make that happen. Judy gives me confidence, especially after our fiasco with the syringe Annie's first night home. I am relieved that we will be able to keep Annie's pain under control by administering the morphine this way.

Mark kisses me goodbye and tells me to call him later. I sit back down beside Annie and stay with her for a while until she goes to sleep.

Mom, Dad and I are gathered around the kitchen table. Upon the advice of the hospice case manager, my parents have already met with the funeral director and have picked out a coffin. Mom gets the folder and shows me the picture of the casket they have decided upon. It is small and white, and is of the new style where half the lid is closed over the bottom of the body and only the top of the body is exposed. The left side of the coffin is the one that opens. Mom has decided she wants Annie to lie on her stomach because she always sleeps on her stomach. Although it was an unusual request, the funeral director says he can honor my mom's wishes.

As I look at the picture of the coffin, though, I realize that if Annie is on her stomach, in this coffin, she will have to have her bent little left arm at the outside and will have to be facing her left arm, or she will have to face away from the visitors. If she faces her right arm, we will not be able to see her face. This is a dilemma for me because to complicate the issue, Annie has been lying on the left side of her face, and as we are not moving her over anymore, she will likely die in this position. I am afraid the left side of her face is going to be disfigured after all of this. I explain my concerns to Mom.

"Do you think the coffin can open from either side?" I ask.

Mom doesn't know, but tells me to call the funeral director about it. I do. He says the best he can do is try to find an older coffin with a lid that opens fully.

My parents have been in a disagreement about what Annie will wear for her laying out at the funeral home.

"I want my girl to have a fancy dress," my dad says. "I want her to look like a princess. She never had a chance to have a pretty dress."

"She should wear her regular clothes," Mom rebuts. "She needs to look like herself."

Throughout the rest of the day I haunt the hallway, periodically peeking into the room to see if Annie is awake. I am terrified she will wake up and be alone. I don't want her to be afraid. I don't know what she is thinking, or how much she understands about what she is going through. She has to know something big is wrong; too many things are different. And she is in pain. I deeply regret it took us as long as it did to figure that out and try to help her, but we're certain of it now.

As hard as we may be trying, we are all crying around her—a lot of the time. Annie picks up on our moods, so I'm sure she understands something sad is going on. I feel bad not being able to prepare her for the way this is going to end. I feel like I am keeping a deep and dark secret from her. The simple matter is I can't know what she is thinking or how much she understands, and there isn't anything I can do about it but hold her hand, talk to her, and just be with her for now so that she is not awake and alone.

When I tiptoe down the hall and peek around the corner into the room, some-times my mom is sitting in the chair beside the bed, stroking Annie's hair, or Carol is sitting in a lotus position on the chair with her eyes closed, meditating, or pray-ing. Sometimes they get up and tell me I can sit down with her, other times I slip quietly away.

My Uncle Tom, Aunt Mary Lou and Uncle Morgan come to visit Annie after dinner. They stand in Annie's room with my parents and talk to her and each other for a little while then leave.

At 8:00 p.m. Rick comes to replace Judy for the night shift. The nurses are working twelve hours around the clock in two shifts. Judy introduces Rick to the family and Annie, then gives him her report and a tour of the house that includes where Annie's medicines are being stored in the refrigerator in the kitchen.

Atropine, to help dry up secretions from her lungs, has been added to the grow-ing list of Annie's medicines. When I talk to the nurses, they seem to be the most concerned about the congestion in Annie's lungs.

I feel like I have been transported into a new dimension. The minutes and hours lose their sharp distinction and blur into a day, a meal, the nighttime. The oxygen generator drones on—a constant reminder.

I have moved my air mattress from the family room to the living room. It is quieter there; Carol says the energy is better in there, and I am closer to the hallway to

Annie's room so I will be able to hear better if something is wrong and Mom needs me.

I wake up in the early hours of the morning and quietly and slowly push the sliding door to the hallway open, then tiptoe down the dark hall and peek into Annie's dim room, where the small lamp on the table glows in the night. Rick is sprawled out in the hard chair beside Annie's bed, with his head leaning against the wall and his eyes closed. He hears me and opens his eyes as he sits up.

"How is she doing?" I whisper.

"She's coughing a little," Rick answers, "and her breaths are short and shallow with some labor. She could use something to help her relax. I've called the hospice doctor to ask for an order for Ativan to help relieve her respiratory distress."

Rick tells me that during the night Annie lifted her head and stared at the headboard of her bed for a while. "Was there something she was looking for?" he asks. I don't know what Annie was thinking, but I think that maybe she became alert and realized something was different about her position in the room. Maybe she was trying to figure out what was going on. I tell him what I think. She is asleep now.

It is so nice to have a medical professional here with us who knows what to do and what Annie needs. The Ativan is already in the house in the Comfort Pak that the hospice nurse supplied our first night home from the hospital. It contains medicines that hospice nurses can administer for comfort, but that require a prescription. Once Rick receives the order over the phone from the hospice doctor he is able to administer the Ativan to Annie, which he does at about 7:00 am. I am so thankful for the hospice nurses. It becomes easy to turn Annie's care over into their hands.

1970s

When I was young I felt cheated. Sometimes I felt cheated out of a younger sister who would look up to me. I looked up to Carol. I watched what she did and tried to emulate her in many ways, from how to wear my hair, to what shoes to buy, pants to wear, or music to listen to.

I didn't have a younger sister I could teach how to do things. I didn't have a younger sister whose hair I could fix or make-up I could put on like my sister did for me. I had a younger sister, but I couldn't do any of those things with her.

I know it sounds small and very self-serving, but the truth is sometimes I just felt like I had been cheated. I felt cheated for myself, and I felt cheated for Annie. We both had been cheated. My mom and dad had been cheated. We all had been cheated out of knowing the person Annie might have been.

Sometimes I wondered if she would have been quieter like me, or vivacious like Carol. Would she have shared a love of reading with me, or would she have been a gifted artist like Carol? What things would we have talked about? My memories of other people all contain conversation. I don't have that for Annie. I have only my words to her and her smiling back at me.

No one ever talked about what we all lost. The closest anyone ever came was when I had interviewed my parents. "How do you think our lives would have been different as a family if Annie would not have been disabled?" I had asked. My dad had answered, " Well, I'd have had one more bright daughter."

He would have. That's what we all were cheated out of.

I never heard my mom utter a word about what might have been. There was no useful point to considering it, and Mom was far too practical to think about it. Or if she ever thought about it, she was too practical to speak of it. But once when I asked if she thought Annie knew she was different, or felt bad that she couldn't do the things that we could do, Mom said, "Look how happy she is. This is the only life she's ever known." Another time Mom said, "In some ways, she's the lucky one. She's never known rejection, or failure, or reprimand. All she's ever known is love."

We loved Annie. She was very special to us. In many ways she was a very special gift to us. We didn't want to deny what she meant to us by wishing she were different. We didn't talk about it.

Would we have magically transformed her into a fully functional human being? In a heartbeat. Not for us, but for her. We had all been cheated—but Annie, by far, had been the most cheated of all.

1980 | *The photographer catches me taking a moment with Annie at my wedding, while my mom watches. Annie is wearing an outfit my mom sewed from the same fabric as the bridesmaids' dresses.*

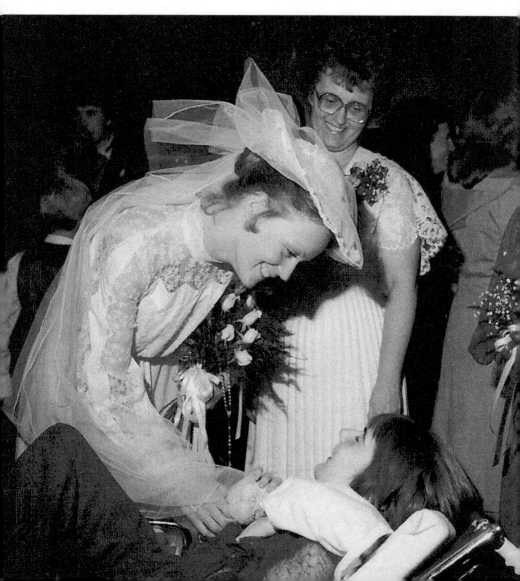

The Lord has promised good to me
His word my hope secures.

He will my shield and portion be,
As long as life endures.

CHAPTER 20 **A Room Full of Angels**

Day 19
Tuesday August 11

The doorbell rings a little before 8:00 in the morning and, while still in my pajamas, I answer the front door that opens into the living room. My air mattress, covered with rumpled bedding, a sheet, a blanket and a pillow, still lies on the floor blocking about half of the open space. My open suitcase is on the floor beside Annie's now-camouflaged wheelchair. The room and I are both a mess and I couldn't care less. Nurse Karen is here to replace Rick.

We've adjusted to the hospice routine much more quickly than I had anticipated, considering that initially my mom resisted help because she didn't want any strangers coming and going at all hours of the day. I think the crisis she and Carol experienced Saturday night made her a convert. Now we have our caseworker Janice checking in periodically, an RN monitoring Annie's condition every few days, a chaplain stopping by, and a hospice nurse here around the clock.

I find comfort in the routine that is repeated each day at 8:00 a.m. and then again at 8:00 p.m. A hospice nurse arrives, introductions are made, departing nurse gives report, gives tour and departs, arriving nurse takes vital signs. I am just plain-out grateful that we have these compassionate, medically competent professionals at Annie's beck and call. The sight of a hospice nurse sitting in the pink recliner in Annie's room, writing in a notebook or reading a book, adds a sense of stability and security to the room. It's a huge contrast from the anxiety we experienced the first night we brought Annie home and were fumbling with the pain medication measurement, or the terror Carol and my parents experienced when Annie couldn't breathe Saturday night and they called for crisis care. The process of dying is very foreign and frightening to me. I don't know what to expect; I don't know how things will go. It's downright terrifying. I really don't know what we would be doing right now without these experienced nurses.

When my mom got up this morning, Rick told her that Annie was awake most of the night. After Rick leaves Mom tells us that when she checked on Annie late last night she found that Rick had turned her over onto her back and elevated her head. "She looked awful," Mom says, "she looked like she was uncomfortable and in pain. I told him to put her back and leave her on her stomach." Annie used to sit up during the day when she was feeling well, but since she is in pain now whenever she gets moved, Mom just wants her to stay on her stomach where she seems to be the most comfortable.

Mom tells me she feels a little bad about being terse with Rick, but she was just reacting to what she saw on Annie's face. Mom understands that the nurses are taught to move patients to prevent bedsores. In Annie's case, the nurses believe she would be able to breathe easier if she were in a different position. But Mom has learned over fifty-one years of caring for her that what is deemed required or optimal care for other people doesn't necessarily apply to Annie. Over the years Mom has had to largely depend on herself when it comes to Annie's care, and she's not about to stop now.

Mom makes it clear to the day nurse Karen that Annie is not to be moved from her stomach.

My parents have still not come to an agreement on what Annie will wear for her funeral. My sister and I decide to go shopping. We know it will be a hardship for Mom or Dad to leave and try to shop for something for Annie to be buried in.

We want to get something pretty. Annie is fifty-one-years old even if she does wear children's sizes. We go to a new shopping area in Dayton and start with the department stores. First we look briefly at dresses and soon realize that they are either childish or too plain. After several failed attempts to find anything we settle on a nightgown. It is a lovely pale pink satin. It is simple with a lacy accent on the front. We realize that no one will see the pretty accent if Annie is lying on her stomach, but the arm has a detail of sheer fabric in overlapping layers that fall over the wrist. It will make Annie's delicate little right hand look beautiful.

At the cash register, the sales clerk is upbeat and says, "This is beautiful, is it a gift for someone?" "It's for our sister," I say and leave it at that. There's no point in ruining this woman's day.

I don't know whether Mom and Dad are happy with our selection or not when we get back. We are all a little disappointed that the lacy accent is on the front and that there is nothing on the back. Mom decides to sew a little lace around the neckline on the back. Later Mom comes into the kitchen with a beautiful small afghan in Easter-egg colors that her mother crocheted. Mom was saving it for her first great-grandchild, but now tells me she is thinking of using it for Annie. I tell her that is a grand idea.

Mom calls Vera, Annie's long-time babysitter, and Christiana to let them know about Annie's condition and invite them to visit her if they'd like.

A few of my parents' friends have stopped by after work to see Annie. They are a group from Mom and Dad's parish who they used to meet at Panera after Mass every Sunday. One man in particular whose name is Bud, like other individuals who have been inexplicably drawn to her over the years, just loves Annie. Bud is a technician at the hospital and works with patients all day; he is still wearing his green scrubs. He has a loud deep voice and a cheerful teasing demeanor.

"I smell something stinky," he says. Mom is standing beside me near the doorway and says softly to me as she chuckles, "He always says that to her." Annie tries to lift her head a little. Bud is standing at the head of the bed leaning over to talk to her. His wife and another woman are standing nearby. Bud is able to get a smile out of Annie. Mom tells me he is one of her favorite people.

I stay in Annie's room after her visitors leave. Someone has placed a child's storybook on the bedside table. It is one of a series of books of short stories that my mom read to us when we were little. She said we used to lie on the floor in a circle and she would read to us. The book strongly evokes childhood memories. Like a song from the past, the scent of the aged pages transports me back to a simpler time where my memories are colored with the songs of mourning doves and the fresh scent of dew on the grass on a crisp spring morning.

Even though Annie's right hand rests motionless, when I slip my hand between hers and the mattress with our palms together, she tightens her fingers around mine and holds on.

Karen tells me it is time for Annie's medicine so I gently remove my hand from Annie's weak grasp, kiss her on the forehead, and stand up to move to the foot of the bed. Karen takes my place by Annie's head and prepares a syringe of medicine, patiently administering it into Annie's mouth a tiny drop at a time placed under her tongue, or in the space between her gum and her cheek.

Karen finishes and places the syringe back in its cup on the nightstand but stays by Annie's side stroking her hair. She wants to make sure Annie keeps the medicine down and doesn't choke on it.

When Annie is resting quietly, a sense of calm and peace descends upon the room transforming it into a holy, almost cathedral-like place. "A few minutes ago Annie was looking over the headboard of her bed and into the corner of the room," Karen says. "I wondered if she was watching an angel."

"Maybe it's my grandmother," I say. Whenever I am in the room with Annie I pray to my deceased relatives, but especially to my Dad's mother because she was a very devout Catholic. Grandma lived beside the church's convent a half a block from her parish, St. Boniface, in Piqua, Ohio. "Grandma," I pray, "please help Annie find her way."

"This room is full of angels," Karen says.

Some people might think that's a little crazy, but I don't. I *want* there to be a room full of angels.

I wake in the night and get up to check on Annie. Nurse Candy has replaced Karen for the night shift. Annie is awake, so I sit with her and hold her hand until she goes back to sleep. I try to sing soft songs, but I struggle because I can't remember all the words. This makes me laugh and then cry. Apparently I only know all the words to two songs, and they are "Down Yonder Green Valley," a song I learned in Girl Scouts that's set to an old Scottish hymn, and "Michael Row the Boat Ashore," both of which I used to sing to my babies in the middle of the night years ago. But that's about the extent of my repertoire. I don't think Annie wants me to keep singing those two songs over and over again. So I decide to hum instead.

As I'm humming, my voice starts to sound stronger and fuller to me. Then it seems as if another voice is blending with mine. It feels magical. I wonder if I am losing my mind. I lift my head and turn towards Candy, who is sitting in the pink recliner, and see that she is softly humming along with me.

In the living room before I lie back down to sleep I find a pen and a scrap of paper and jot down the words that are running through my mind:

> *I have a little sister whose name is Annie*
> *I felt her love in her sweet smile*
> *Whenever I bent to kiss her face.*
>
> *I have a little Angel whose name is Annie*
> *I feel her presence wrap me with love*
> *When I close my eyes to sleep.*

I have a little sister angel whose name is Annie.
She dances in heaven and waits for me.

1970s

The trick to putting Annie to bed was getting yourself lined up right in the beginning. I maneuvered Annie's chair beside her bed with the head of her chair at the foot of the bed. This didn't seem intuitive, but it was the way it worked. I stood between her bed and her chair.

"Okay, Annie. I'm going to pick you up now." She laughed, but it was a nervous laugh. She was a little worried about me picking her up; I didn't do it very often.

"Don't worry. I know exactly what I'm doing," I said.

I pulled up on her right arm, bent over her, and worked my left arm underneath her shoulders, trying to get it all the way across her back where I could grip her other shoulder in my hand. I worked my right arm under her legs. Still bent over her chair, I curled my arms containing her close to my chest, stood up, turned around 180 degrees, and bent over her bed, dropping to the mattress with her in my arms. She laughed a nervous and relieved laugh this time. She knew she had made it safely to bed.

"See. I told you not to worry," I said.

I talked her through the whole nighttime routine as I worked. First I removed her pants and changed her diaper. Then I put her pajama bottoms on, tugging them up over her hips. I had to do a side-to-side movement as I rolled her hip up and tugged and then repeated on the other side. When I took her shirt off, I remembered to take her flexible right arm out first and then her stiff left one. I did the opposite when I put her pajamas top on. The left arm went in first. It made the whole exercise so much easier.

"There," I said. "Over you go." I pulled her closer to the edge of the bed, and then gently rolled her towards the wall so she would be on her stomach. She immediately popped her head up to look around. I arranged her left arm so that it was flat and tucked comfortably beneath her, then I checked her legs to make sure the right one was on top of the left. I got the hairbrush from the night table and gently stroked it through her hair as she lay on her cheek facing me. Finally, using both of my hands and working from my shoulders, I gave her a strong backrub to work the tightness out of her little curved back. I could almost feel her sigh of relief as she melted under my hands.

"That feels good, doesn't it Sweetheart?" I said. She tried to pop her head back up, but I gently pressed it back down. "Lay your head-y down. It's time to go to sleep." I pulled the cover up over her back. "Good night Sweetheart," I said. I kissed her goodnight, turned the light off, and left the room.

2000 | *Annie rests at a roadside park during a trip south for vacation.*

CHAPTER 21 **Signs of Death**

Day 20
Wednesday August 12

I wake up early and go into Annie's room first thing. Candy is still here, and she looks tired and like she needs to go to bed. I am so grateful the hospice nurses are carrying the night vigil with Annie for us, so that we are all able to sleep. What we are going through would be so many times worse if we were sleep deprived at the same time. I am especially grateful that my parents are able to sleep at night.

When I ask Candy how Annie is doing, she tells me about Annie's vital signs and that there may be some mottling beginning to appear on the right hand. I don't have any idea what this means, but I know that in addition to keeping Annie comfortable, and answering our family's questions and supporting our emotional needs, the hospice nurses also look for signs of impending death.

"What is mottling?" I ask.

Candy explains to me that the dying body begins to shut down circulation to the extremities to conserve the blood flow to the vital organs like the heart and brain.

Mottling is a term for red and blue splotches that appear on the hands and feet when that starts to happen.

I realize I know little to nothing about what happens to the body as we die, and I want to know more about the dying process. I want to be able to prepare myself. I want to be able to watch Annie and warn myself. Knowing what might happen takes away some of the fear for me about what is going to happen or why something has happened.

At the 8:00 a.m. shift change Andrea arrives. Andrea is younger than the other nurses have been, and maybe that's the reason she seems to be a little nervous or lacking in confidence. I'm getting a distinct impression that Annie's situation is more than Andrea had bargained for, whether it is because of Annie's cerebral palsy or state of decline due to the cancer. Andrea leaves the room and seeks my mom out throughout the day to consult or to ask for assistance with Annie. I actually feel kind of bad for her to be put in this situation for which she seems somehow unprepared. It makes me appreciate the stoicism and aplomb the other nurses have shown as they've dealt with Annie's care and impending death.

I'm trying to keep tabs on Annie's vital signs by asking the nurses, although I don't know how to fully interpret what I hear. The nurses offer me patient explanations. Annie's respirations are at about 18/minute when she is comfortable and at rest. They accelerate to somewhere in the 20s/minute when she is in pain. Her respirations are a very helpful indicator for Annie's pain medication needs.

I am sitting beside Annie while she sleeps when she opens her eyes and starts to dry heave. I ask Andrea to go and get my mom. She returns with Mom who gives Annie a phenergan suppository for nausea. After about a half hour Annie calms down and has her eyes closed again.

Although Mom still tries to help with Annie's care at times, mostly the nurses are managing it. Mom wanders through the house seemingly without purpose now that she's not feeding, changing and dressing Annie. Sometimes she sits in the living room by the window with a needle and thread and sews lace on the nightgown for Annie.

My dad spends a lot of time in his bedroom. He seems to be uncomfortable in Annie's room. I suspect, like the rest of us, he can't bear to see her suffer like this. I also think he would like to be able to pick her up and hold her. Before this illness, he picked her up every day to move her from her bed to her chair and back. He has expressed a desire to pick her up. But since she is in obvious pain when she's moved, and now she's connected to the oxygen, no one is encouraging him, or allowing him, to lift her. Carol has told Dad that he needs to try to come and sit by Annie sometimes. Annie would want him to be there.

Earlier today Mark called me to tell me he is coming up to spend the night with me tonight. I ask him to bring the printer for my computer, photo paper, and spare ink.

I have started thinking about preparing photo boards for Annie's funeral. I have most of the photos I need on my computer, and the ones I don't have I will scan at Mom's house.

When Mark arrives, I set up the printer next to my computer on my dad's desk in the family room. It is a large executive's desk that he bought when he still had his tool & die business. I have a photo of Dad sitting at this desk at his company, Martin Palmer Tool & Die, with Annie sitting beside him in her wheelchair, when she used to go to work with them during the years my mom took care of the office work there.

Mark also brings me some changes of clothes as my aborted Maine vacation supply is running out. We inflate a second twin-size air mattress for Mark to sleep on that completely blocks off the floor space in the living room when placed beside mine.

Sometime in the early hours of morning I wake up and sneak into Annie's room to check on her. The night nurse Joanne tells me my mom was just in here. Annie is sleeping quietly, so I go back to bed.

1960s–1970s

Both of my parents carried Annie everywhere when she was young. My mom was my Girl Scout leader. She took Annie with us to the neighborhood park where the meetings were held in a park building. She carried Annie from the house to the car. We didn't have a car seat for Annie at the time, and in the 60's, seatbelts weren't even readily available. Mom sat Annie up in middle of the front seat, and like bookends, Mom and I sat on either side of her and kept her erect between us. When we got to the park, Mom carried Annie into the building where she laid her on the sofa while the Girl Scouts met.

When I was still pretty young, Mom wanted to visit the neighbor who lived across the alley from our house on the outskirts of the small town of Piqua, Ohio. It was winter, so Mom must have bundled both Annie and me up in our coats. Then she picked Annie up and proceeded to walk through our back yard and across the alley. The ground was covered with snow. When we got into the neighbor's yard, Mom fell with Annie. She was cradling Annie in both of her arms in front, and she must have slipped on the snow. She fell forward onto her knees and down to her bent arms holding Annie. I don't remember what happened, or how Mom got up. All I remember is that when Mom fell, I got very scared, until she started laughing. Holding Annie while on the ground, Mom didn't know how she was going to get back up, and she started to laugh at the predicament she had gotten herself into.

One time we had a wheelchair accident. We were on vacation, touring Washington D.C. and had just gotten into the Capital Building when dad decided to take Annie down the escalator in her homemade wheel chair. My mom of course put up resistance, but sometimes there was no stopping my dad when he got on a roll. Dad demonstrated why there are now signs all over escalators warning people not to get on with a stroller or wheelchair. Annie's wheel got caught, my dad stumbled and ended up sitting right down on his butt on one of the steps as he held tight to the handles of Annie's tipped-back chair. Fortunately, the wheel was the only casualty. I was in front of them on the escalator. I heard my mom shout, "Jerry!" I turned around just in time to see him sit down on the step, pulling Annie's chair with him. We had to spend the rest of the afternoon procuring replacement wheels from a bike shop and then waiting on the hot sidewalk in the sun while my dad repaired Annie's chair. We never did get to see the Capital Building. We did however get to take a tour of D.C. in a taxi, which was a thrill for us, and something we would never have spent the money on if not for the escalator incident.

Another time Mom was carrying Annie upstairs to bed and Annie reached out with her strong right hand and grabbed the railing. With both of her arms full of Annie, Mom had little choice but to sit down on the steps and wait for help. That was only a near miss and not a fall. It may, however, have been the impetus for our family to move to a single-story house.

One day when Dad was home alone with Annie, he stumbled down the last few steps to the basement carrying her. Our garage was in the basement at that house, and Dad was in a hurry, trying to respond to a family member who had a personal emergency. Dad created an emergency of his own that day. When Mom got home from the store, she was greeted by an ambulance parked in front of the house. Dad was fine, but Annie's leg was broken. My dad could tell, by Annie's flinch and her facial expression, that she was in pain when he touched her leg. Annie went to the hospital and got a cast. She still swung her leg around, cast and all, and took it all in stride, although Mom said the noise from the saw they used when it came time to remove the cast scared Annie.

When Annie got older and heavier, my mom still lifted her in her arms from the bed to her chair and back again. Eventually, once my dad retired, Mom quit doing that and let Dad take care of the lifting.

Even when Dad was 76 years old, he lifted Annie in his arms until the day she went to the hospital, August 1, 2009.

With all this pushing, carrying, and lifting, I suppose we were lucky there weren't more accidents than the few that we had.

circa mid-1960s | Dad holds Annie upright for a photo.

CHAPTER 22 **An Instinct to Die**

Day 21

Thursday August 13

I get up as soon as I wake and watch for the nurse so that the doorbell won't ring and disturb Annie. I see Karen, our hospice nurse from Tuesday, walking around the sidewalk from the driveway to our front door. She looks like an old friend to me and I am happy she's back, but also surprised. On Tuesday when she was here, Karen told my sister that she requests to only be placed in adult patients' homes. She explained that she had a daughter who died when she was ten-years old in a similar manner where there were days spent at her bedside. She said she asked to not be assigned to children because it is too difficult emotionally for her. She was assigned to take care of Annie because, by most standards, Annie is an adult at fifty-one. But by a practical standard that really counts, Annie is a child. She is cared for as a child. On Tuesday when Karen was here it was obvious that her maternal instincts were kicking in with Annie's care. She sat by Annie's bed and talked to her and stroked her hair and rubbed her back. I suspect it may have been difficult for her to relive the loss of her own child this way.

"You came back!" I say in greeting when I open the door to Karen.

"I asked to," she responds.

Karen is just one more example of how Annie touches hearts and brings out the goodness in other people.

Before she leaves, the night nurse Joanne tells Karen that Annie is having difficulty tolerating her Phenobarbital and Dilantin liquids because they are making her nauseated. These are the two medicines that my parents have been giving Annie faithfully every day since she was first diagnosed with cerebral palsy in 1959 and started having seizures. They are Annie's lifelines.

Karen calls Dr. Richards and requests Dilantin that can be administered rectally, additionally Dr. Richards tells her it is okay to stop the Phenobarbital. Annie is taking so many different medicines for comfort right now that I can't keep track of them. She gets Atropine for secretions and Ativan for anxiety. Oxycodone is for pain. Annie wears something they call a Scop patch for nausea and vomiting, and another patch that is for pain. She also gets phenergan for nausea. The nurses are vigilant about making sure Annie is comfortable. Karen also rubs lotions on Annie's upper and lower extremities. She uses one of the green sponges dipped in water to moisten Annie's lips.

The hospice nurses have seemed a little surprised that Annie is still with us given the condition of her lungs based on the audible sounds of congestion and the effort it appears to take for her to draw a breath. She looks like she is using every muscle in her torso to heave her rib cage open and draw in air, without rest. The nurses also continue to note the mottling on Annie's hands.

It is exhausting to watch her body struggle to stay alive. "Please help her," I pray. At fifty-one, Annie is relatively young and her heart is strong. Her heart pumps with a survival instinct to live, live. Her back and chest muscles strain to work her lungs to breathe, breathe. I am powerless as I stand beside her willful organs and whisper, "Let go, Sweetheart. Rest now."

My dad knows we have begun to make preparations for Annie's impending funeral. We've had conversations about coffins. Flowers have been picked out.

Carol showed me a eulogy that she drafted. Mom is sewing lace on a nightgown.

Dad and I are sitting at the table getting ready for lunch, when he announces, "I've got something I want to say." And he starts to dictate a short little poem he has created in his mind. I rush to find a paper and pen to transcribe as he speaks,

> *God gave her to us for what time she had,*
> *and with His help we did the best we could.*
> *Now He'd like to have her back.*
> *She touched many lives while she was here.*

The funeral director has asked us to find a quote from the Bible we would like to use on the back of Annie's prayer cards. We decide to use these words from my father instead.

Carol went shopping at the craft store and returns home with four pink foam core poster boards to use for Annie's photo display at the funeral visitation. She also has some artificial orchids in whites, and pastel and vibrant shades of pink. When I am not sitting with Annie I am at the desk in the family room editing and printing photos and photo captions. Carol has set up two card tables in the center of the room and puts a piece of foam core on one and tools and supplies on the other—scissors, Elmer's glue, hot glue, a measuring stick and straight-edge.

We work together on this project. I provide the technical details, and Carol dictates the aesthetics. I choose the photo and caption, and Carol determines the size and placement on the poster. I print the items out and Carol trims and attaches them to the board. It reminds me of when we were young and the many projects we worked on together. In particular I think of the year she and I created stained-glass windows, out of colored tissue paper and black construction paper, that completely covered two of the windows on the first floor of our house. One was a picture of three candles burning with flames and the other was the Christmas star.

My mom stops through the family room periodically and looks at the pictures we have spread out on the desk and tables. She expresses which ones she likes.

Occasionally she shares a memory a photo sparks. My dad sits on the love seat between the desk and the table Carol is working on and just watches us and listens to what we are saying. The atmosphere in the room is celebratory of Annie's life, and what she's meant to us, and is filled with a sense of purpose. In our focus on presenting a wonderful and fitting tribute to our sister, we are able to forget temporarily that she lies dying in the room down the hall.

Annie has started having trouble with secretions that fill her mouth and then spill onto her bed. She tries to clear her throat. It is horrible to watch her struggle like this. She looks at us with what sometimes seems like pleading eyes asking, "Someone help me, please." We try to comfort her as best we can.

From the beginning Mom has placed a small soft towel under the side of Annie's face so that we can change it easily if medicines are spilled or it gets wet from some kind of body fluid. Mom has about five or six of these very soft towels in bright colors of yellow, fuchsia, blue, green and teal that she bought for Annie a while back.

We are going through the towels pretty quickly now in our efforts to keep Annie's resting place dry and comfortable, and we are down to the last towel. Mom is trying to wash and dry them in the laundry, but there just aren't enough for this almost non-stop leakage and regurgitation of frothy light brown liquid. I suggest that maybe we should cut the towels into smaller pieces to place just under Annie's mouth thereby multiplying how many we have. Mom doesn't want to destroy the nice towels. She leaves the room and comes back with a pair of scissors and the pillowcase that matches Annie's soft flannel sheets. She sits down and systematically cuts the pillowcase into many 4-inch squares that she stacks in a neat pile on the dresser in Annie's room.

I wonder where all this fluid is coming from, and Karen tells me it may be from Annie's lungs that have been filling up with liquid. Lying on her stomach has not helped this situation.

Karen sees that Annie is struggling to keep her throat clear, so late in the afternoon she makes a call to the Hospice magic place where the medicines and supplies come from and soon a suction machine is delivered to the house. She sets it up on the bedside table and gently suctions the phlegm out of the back of Annie's mouth. This machine is a Godsend. Annie is able to rest quietly after Karen finishes.

I have a conversation with Karen about yesterday's day nurse, Andrea. I tell her that Andrea didn't seem to have a lot of confidence, or even to really know what to do at times. Karen, a long-time hospice veteran, says she is not familiar with Andrea. She thinks Andrea may be an agency nurse who has been enlisted to help out and not an actual hospice nurse. This is important information to me because of the whole hospice philosophy and the do-not-resuscitate orders. Some of the hospice nurses have struggled with our dictates for Annie's care regarding not moving her from her position on her stomach. When Andrea was here it seemed we had to remind her when it was time for Annie's pain medicines. Some nurses have the philosophy with patients that you only administer meds as needed for pain. Here again, Annie is not able to tell people when her meds are needed until she is in so much pain she is grinding her teeth and blowing out her cheeks. We want the meds administered on a regularly scheduled basis. There is simply no reason not to.

As Karen uses the suction machine on Annie again, she tells me she is concerned that if we get another non-hospice/agency nurse he or she may not know how to use the suction machine correctly.

"Can you teach me how, so that at least I may be able to show someone else?" I ask her, thinking that it doesn't look that complicated. As she works, Karen explains the steps involved in using the machine and how to prevent hurting Annie's mouth with the suction. I know enough that I may be able to do something in a crisis situation, but I hope I don't have to.

"You can request that only hospice nurses be sent to take care of Annie," Karen tells me. "Just let your case worker know."

I tell Mom, and she asks Janice about this when she comes.

Janice confirms that Annie is showing some signs that she is progressing towards death. Janice tells us that whenever we leave Annie's room, we should be sure to tell her goodbye because, even with the best of intentions, there is no way to predict exactly how or when her death will occur.

Christiana, Annie's caregiver for the past several months, stops by in the evening to visit Annie. She sits by her side and quietly talks to Annie for a long time. When she leaves she asks my mom if she can come back again.

I wake up and slip into Annie's room in the wee hours of the morning. Her toy hand-held mirror lies above her right hand just out of reach. Someone must have placed it there when she could no longer hold it. Her hand lies still on the mattress. It is a beautiful and graceful little hand. When I sit down and stroke her hair, and start talking to her, her hand lies motionless on the mattress, but she raises her little finger in greeting. It's all the strength she has. It breaks my heart.

Someone has placed Annie's opal ring back on her finger. I think they took it off at the hospital, but Mom must have put it back on sometime yesterday. I look at her little hand lying so still on the mattress. I look at the three delicate gold chain bracelets that I wear on my left wrist and never take off. I unclasp the lightest and oldest one that I've worn for years and gently place it around Annie's right wrist. Her arm is so tiny that a length of the gold chain pools to the mattress. If she were to sit up and use her arm, this bracelet would fall right off. It looks pretty and delicate decorating my little sister's arm. Annie has her eyes open, but it doesn't seem like she can see me anymore. I gently tug on the bracelet so she will know it is there and tell her, "You have a beautiful bracelet now, Annie." I don't really know if she even realizes I gave it to her, but it makes me feel better to see her still hand wearing it.

I lean close to her face and whisper my litany to her.

"Mom loves you.

"Dad loves you.

"Carol loves you.

"I love you.

"Everybody loves you.

"Everybody knows you love us too."

I know that people tell stories about encouraging their loved ones to "Go to the light," when they are dying, or to "Let go." I've been telling Annie the same. I tell her, "Go to the light, Sweetheart. Look for Grandma. Look for Uncle Mike and Aunt Nancy. Do you see Grandma? You go when you're ready." But it presses on me that she might not know what that means.

I turn to Joanne who sits silently in the pink recliner by the little light that throws the room into a soft glow. "What can I tell her?" I ask. "I don't know if she evens knows what it means to go to the light." Joanne reassures me that it is instinctual to know how to die. "Tell her it's okay to die," she says.

I turn back to Annie with my head resting against hers and I whisper, "It's okay to," but I am unable to say the word die.

2008

One day when I was visiting in the early 1990s, I was sitting beside Annie with my arms leaning on the rail of her chair and my hands hanging above her body, a position all of us frequently took with her. She placed the fingers of her right hand on my left and started gently touching my hand and feeling across it, as if she were seeing it with her fingers in a manner akin to the blind. When she discovered my diamond engagement ring this way, she dwelt on it, examining it thoroughly with the whisper soft touch of her fingers and thumb. "That's my pretty ring, Annie," I said. "Would you like to see it?" I took it off my hand and placed it on the middle finger of her right hand. She responded by lifting her hand as if to admire it and closing and opening her fingers. "You like my pretty ring, don't you, Sweetheart?" I said.

It dawned on me that Annie was a woman, not a child anymore, and that although infant toys were still the only things you could safely give her without concern that she might hurt herself from hard edges, or cut off the blood circulation in her finger because she got it stuck, she might like something more adult-like.

At home I had an old opal ring I received from a boyfriend in college that I never wore anymore. I decided to give it to Annie for Christmas. When I helped her unwrap the present and placed the ring on her finger, she was excited to get it, but then she was always excited to get any kind of present. I think she just liked the festive atmosphere, the noise of the paper, and the attention.

She wore that opal ring every day. Dad would often say to her, "Show me your ring," and she would hold her hand up with her fingers extended as if she were admiring it.

Because we included her in our conversations, Annie was also not immune to the teasing that runs rampant in our family, especially amongst my dad's siblings. Aunt Mary Lou often enters a room with high energy and a boisterous voice. When she visited, after she greeted Annie with a lively hello, Aunt Mary Lou always said, "I'm going to get your ring," in a teasing, threatening voice. Annie would respond by clamping her hand down into a fist and moving her arm up and down, "Oh no, you're not," she'd "say."

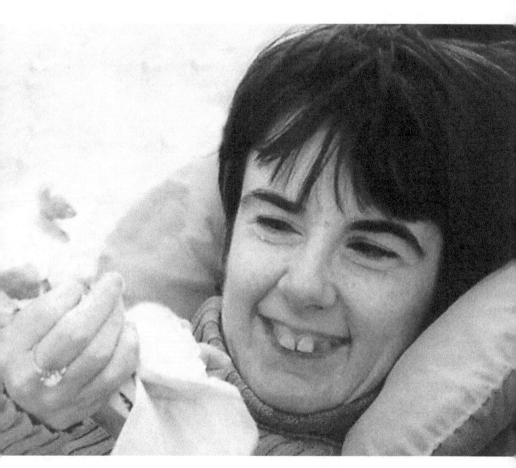

2000 | *Annie holds a piece of wrapping paper she tore from a package she was helping unwrap at my Mom's birthday party.*

CHAPTER 23 **Let's Go Fly a Kite**

Day 22
Friday August 14

In the afternoon Carol and I get in trouble with the nurse. After lunch I am in the room with Annie trying to sing "Let's Go Fly a Kite" from her favorite movie Mary Poppins. I'm not overly exuberant, but let's face it; it is not a calm and quiet song. Carol comes into the room and joins me. Annie has her eyes open, and we are in our entertaining-Annie mode. The song gets louder. Carol says, "Annie is probably tired of all this doom and gloom in here. She likes it when we are happy. It feels more normal to her." Annie is not laughing or even smiling, but she is keeping her sightless eyes open.

When I leave the room the day nurse, whose name is Susan, gets up from the pink recliner where she's been observing and follows me out into the hall. "Can I talk to you for a minute?" she asks.

"Of course."

"I don't want to step on anybody's toes," she says, "but I think your sister Annie needs a calm and quiet atmosphere now. It's best not to be too loud in her room, and maybe only play calm and soothing light music."

I think, But Annie likes it when we entertain her. I think, This is how we always are with Annie. I think, We like to cheer Annie up. I want to be allowed to have the relationship with Annie I've always had, and I feel like this nurse is taking that away from me. Then I realize that Annie's death is taking that away from me.

Susan explains, "Loudness startles Annie back to reality, and that causes an increased need for medication to maintain her comfort."

I remember that we are here to help Annie die, not to keep her with us. I say, "I'm sorry. I understand. I'll tell Carol."

circa 1970

I was at home babysitting Annie, and we were listening to the radio, when the song "Windy" by the Association came on.

"Annie! It's our favorite song," I yelled as I jumped up, grabbed an imaginary microphone, and started singing out loud along with the radio, in front of her chair. I replaced the name "Windy" with "Annie."

I started marching to the beat of the words, "Da da, bum bum bum bum."

Annie got excited and started waving her right arm up and down. She had a big grin on her face. I had a captivated audience, and now I was in full swing. I ran over and jumped onto the sofa, still holding my imaginary microphone in my right hand and using big dramatic arm motions with my left. I was singing out loud. Emphasis on the loud.

I jumped back off the sofa, got behind Annie's chair, and twirled her in a circle as I sang. Annie was laughing all the while. By the time the song was over I was short of breath, and I had worked Annie into state of utter excitement.

"We love that song, don't we Annie?" I said. "Whew!" I collapsed to the floor, arms and legs flaying out from my sides in an exhausted position, going for one more chuckle from Annie.

She complied.

1998 | Carol, Annie and me, celebrating Annie's 40th birthday.

Yea, when this flesh and heart shall fail,
And mortal life shall cease,

I shall possess within the veil,
A life of joy and peace.

CHAPTER 24 **Candlelight Parades**

Day 23

Saturday August 15

I get up in the night and go to Annie's room. I whisper, "How is she doing?" The night nurse Lisa tells me that her breathing is slowing down. I can see this for myself. Annie's breaths are audible and visible with her heaving ribcage. It is not difficult to time them. I watch the clock and count Annie's breaths for several minutes. She is taking about 11 breaths a minute.

I sit down in the chair beside her bed and place my hand on top of hers. She has stopped holding on to our hands.

I think it would be nice if I could pray the rosary. Even though I am not what anyone would consider a devout Catholic, there have been times when I have found comfort in the chant-like prayers of the rosary. I know my dad was praying the rosary in Annie's room at night before she went to the hospital. I look around the room to see if he left a rosary in here somewhere. But I don't see one.

"Do you happen to have a rosary in your bag?" I ask Lisa.

"No one has ever asked me that before," she says. "I probably should have one."

I decide I can try to say the rosary without the beads. I try, but without something to keep track on it is difficult to pray ten Hail Mary's and not lose count. Then I notice the green ribbon bows tied on Annie's handrail across her bed. I get up, walk around the bed and untie one. While returning to my chair I begin to tie ten small knots in the ribbon. I use the ribbon to pray the rosary softly by Annie's bedside.

When I am finished I count Annie's breaths again and they are down to ten a minute. Her respirations have been steadily declining throughout the night.

"At what point do you call the family in?" I ask Lisa.

"Usually at about eight breaths a minute," she replies.

I wait a little longer and then decide to go back to bed. I trust that Lisa will wake me when it's time.

At about 4:30 a.m. the sound of the door to the hallway sliding open wakes me up. Lisa leans over my bed on the floor and gently tells me, "I am going to wake up Carol and your parents."

We all gather in Annie's room. We are still wearing our pajamas. I have been praying for Annie to be released from this suffering for days. But at the same time, I know that death is final, and there is some comfort in the fact that her little body is still warm and breathing, labored though it be. I've never been with someone when they died and I don't know what to expect. It's all very surreal.

Mom is sitting in the chair, resting her head on the bed beside Annie's. My dad sits in a chair we've moved beside Mom's, and I am sitting in a chair beside him. Carol is sitting on the other side of the bed and appears to be in deep meditation. I'm counting Annie's breaths and I think they are at about six a minute.

I am quivering on the inside.

My dad looks lost. I ask him if he would like to pray the rosary with me. I go into my parents' bedroom where I've been instructed the rosaries are hanging on the back of the door and bring back two.

"Hail Mary," I say and Dad joins in, "full of grace, the Lord is with thee."

We continue on with this. When we are finished I count Annie's breaths again and they are at about eight a minute. Her breaths are going back up.

I catch Lisa's eyes and whisper, "Are we going the wrong direction?"

"Sometimes people will rouse when their family members are present," Lisa explains. "She loves you so much; she may be trying to stay here with you." She says, "Sometimes if the family leaves the room the patient will pass on."

We think Annie may be hanging on for us so we decide to leave the room. We all say our goodbyes and gather at the kitchen table while we wait. The sun is rising and there's still no word from Lisa who keeps vigil at Annie's side. It's 8:00 and the day nurse Donna has arrived. Annie is still with us.

After she gets the report and Lisa leaves, Donna comes into the kitchen and says, "Come back in here with Annie, if you want to. People will go when they are ready to."

Annie's long-time babysitter Vera comes to visit her this afternoon.

Mark brings three of our young-adult children to have dinner with me and to visit Annie. The boys, Matt and Joe, are timid and peek into the doorway to Annie's room for a few moments and then return to the living room. My daughter Anna steps into the room with me, but stops in the middle while I walk over to Annie and stroke her hair.

Throughout the week, friends have brought food over to the house for us to eat. Tonight my Aunt MaryLou stops over with a red velvet cake. We invite her to join us and are all sitting at the dining room table when Donna comes out. "I want to tell you a story before I leave," she says.

"There was a little boy who died and went to heaven. His mother was inconsolable. She cried and cried and cried every day. Meanwhile, every day in heaven the angels led all the little children in a parade. This was a very big event and all the children were excited to participate. The angels gave each child a candle, and then set it aglow with a bright flame. But this little boy was sad because he couldn't walk with a light in the parade. His mother's tears kept extinguishing his candle's flame."

May 2006

A few years ago I made a quick trip to Dayton to have lunch with some friends and wanted to stop by for a short visit with my parents.

I surprised my mom with my visit. "Come in, come in, and sit down for a minute," she said. " Your dad should be home soon; he just ran over to the store for some milk."

We walked into the kitchen and I hung my purse over a chair. "Where's Annie?"

"I put her in bed for her afternoon rest."

I walked through the kitchen into the dining room calling out, "Annie, where are you?" As I moved through the hallway to her bedroom doorway, I called again, "Annie…" and stepped into her room.

Music was coming from the stereo on her dresser. It was the Barry Manilow CD I gave her for Christmas. Annie was reclining in her hospital bed along the opposite wall of the room. She was looking straight ahead and not at the doorway, but she was sitting perfectly still and listening intently. Her frail left arm was folded tightly into her chest and looked a bit like a chicken wing. Her right arm was poised about eighteen inches above her face. She grasped an infant's hand-held mirror toy between her thumb and the palm of her hands, the rest of her fingers were stretched out and extended as if she were admiring a new manicure.

She looked over at me as I entered the room. "There you are, Annie," I said as I approached the bed. "You didn't know I was coming, did you?" I brushed her bangs to the side, leaned over the aluminum bed rail, and kissed her on the forehead." Annie started to open and close her fingers on her right hand. She closed her fingers in a trill, one finger at a time, starting with the baby finger in a very quick but smooth and flowing motion. Then she began to twist her wrist up and down in a rhythmic fashion. She was smiling with a big wide, open-mouthed smile and started to chuckle—a low sound that came from deep in her throat. She quickly looked over at me with her deep brown, nearly black, eyes and then coyly looked away again.

"You have your pretty ring on," I said. Still leaning over the bed, I held her right hand around the toy and said a few more things to her, and then I told her, "I'm going out to the kitchen now to talk to mom. I'll come back and say goodbye before I leave." I joined Mom in the kitchen and we sat at the table having a conversation. Barry Manilow was singing softly from Annie's room through the intercom that sat on the kitchen counter.

Dad came home while I was still there and after he said hello to me, he called out, "Where's my girl?" Mom told him Annie had laid down long enough, so he could get her up now if he wanted to. He went back to her bedroom and lifted Annie from her bed to her chair. We could hear him talking to her over the intercom.

"Did you get up, Annie?" I asked as my dad pushed her chair into the kitchen and parked it by the doorway. She smiled, looked shyly to the side, and swung her wrist up and down.

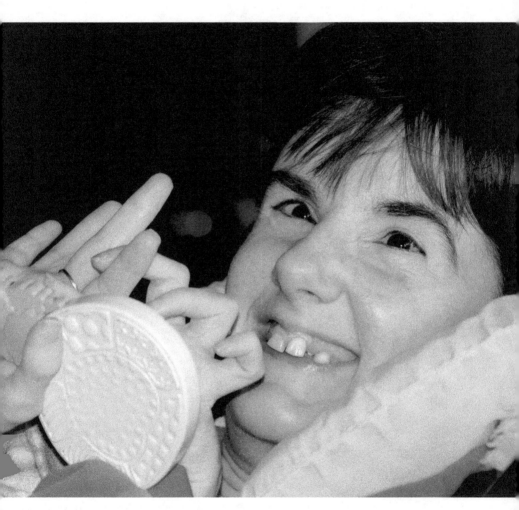

2008 | Annie smiling at me.

CHAPTER 25

A Cloud Burst

Day 24

Sunday August 16

I get up in the middle of the night and check on Annie. The skin on her face has a bluish tinge around her mouth. Her right hand is motionless; it is cool to the touch. I check her feet under the sheet that covers her and they too are cool. I pick up the afghan that is on the chest in her room and gently drape it over her legs to her waist.

Michelle comes to replace our night nurse Lisa at 8:00 a.m. Annie is no longer responsive, but rests peacefully without any sign of pain or distress.

I get ready and take Dad to Mass at 9:30. He goes to Mass faithfully every week, and my mom thinks it will do him good to get out of the house for an hour or two. I have my cell phone. We can be back quickly if we need to.

We have a little scuffle before we leave because Dad wants to bring Annie's wheelchair. I don't know whether he feels like that is part of his identity and people won't know who he is without it, or if he wants to bring it to let the community know Annie is sick, or maybe it is just some strange twisted symptom of the lack of judgment in a mind with dementia. I am able to talk him out of it.

After Mass I take Dad to his favorite place to eat—Golden Nugget Pancake House. We both order a hefty breakfast of omelets and pancakes. Dad gets a little teary-eyed at times, but mostly we have a pleasant experience.

When we walk back outside to go home, Dad looks up at the sky and says, "It's going to rain today." I look up and see that the sky is a brilliant blue, dotted with white puffy cotton-ball clouds. I don't know why he thinks it is going to rain.

I spend the rest of the day working on the posters with Carol and taking breaks to check on, or sit with, Annie for a few minutes. She is completely unresponsive. I still feel the need to whisper as if I might disturb her sleep, but the nurse and my mom are using their full voices in the room and Annie doesn't stir.

It is close to dinner time. My sister is preparing a meal for us. My parents are in and out of the kitchen, milling about. The mood is calm.

I look outside and see that it is raining. It is a real downpour—a cloudburst that happened all of a sudden. Dad's prediction was right.

The table is set and we're going to eat in just a few minutes, but I feel a need to make a quick check on Annie. Maybe it's because I'm feeling bad that she is in her room by herself while we are gathered here in the dining room. So many times before when Mom was preparing the meal, she asked one of us to go tell everybody it's time to eat and bring Annie out here. I would walk into the family room where other family members were watching TV; Annie would be sitting at an angle to the side and front of the television where she could see it but wouldn't be blocking everyone's view. "Hey, Annie," I would say, "you've got to come out here with me." And then I would navigate her chair through the door-way and living room, and park it in the wide doorway to the dining room, so she would be near the table and could watch us and listen to our conversation.

Periodically, someone would shout out to her to pull her into the conversation,

"Where's my girl?" my dad would boom.

"Annie, I see you over there," I'd say.

Annie acknowledged our comments by bending up her right knee and extending her foot back out, or lifting her right arm up and down. She might smile; she might chuckle; she might even holler as if she were trying to respond verbally.

I feel bad today that she is in her room alone. I only have a few minutes before dinner, so I hurry through the doorways and hallway into her room and stand beside her bed.

As I stand guard beside her, I watch Annie's pulse fluttering rapidly in her neck, through the carotid artery the nurse explained earlier. Annie's labored breathing, which I have become accustomed to hearing, shifts in some way.

"How is she doing?" I ask.

Michelle gets up and stands across the bed from me. "Her breaths are shallow," Michelle says, "but I haven't heard any apnea yet."

"What is apnea?" I ask.

Annie holds her breath for a moment.

"It's like that," Michelle responds.

After the false alarm at 4:30 a.m. yesterday when the night nurse Lisa woke us and we all gathered in Annie's room, the hospice nurses seem reluctant to make any dire predictions.

"I think you should go and get my mom," I say.

Michelle hurries out of the room.

The house takes on a dreamlike quality. I hear my mom's voice as if muffled and from a distance shouting, "Christine!" She doesn't realize I'm in here. I can't respond with a call because I don't want to disturb Annie. And I can't leave Annie's side because my feet are rooted to the floor.

Alone in the room with her, I don't take my eyes from Annie's visible heartbeat that flutters, then shifts into one, two, three deep pulses, and then stops. It takes me a moment to realize the sound of her breathing is also gone, as is she.

"Goodbye little sister angel," I whisper. "I'll be looking for you."

After 11 days of listening to her labored breathing and watching her thin rib cage heave with each breath, the relief is immense that she is now at rest—and so is the sorrow.

CHAPTER 26 **Dancing in Heaven**

August 16, 2010

For Annie's obituary I wrote, " Annie never walked, she never spoke, and she never worked. She filled our lives with smiles, and radiated light and love every day of her life." So little I could say about her, yet so much.

I can't explain why Annie had to die the way she did. I can't explain why she lived.

For weeks after Annie's death I still tried to make sense of it. I tried to understand somehow, some way, what it all meant.

Shortly after Annie's death, in a fit of despair, my father said, "Fifty-one years we took care of her and it was all for nothing."

"Oh no, Dad," I said, "how can you say that?" I don't believe that is the truth of his feelings but only a momentary expression of anguish at having lost this precious life that he and my mother had largely devoted their lives to nurturing.

I can't explain any of it. All I know is that there is something inside of me because Annie did live.

Throughout my childhood I felt special—not necessarily always in a positive way—but special nevertheless. I never fully realized how special we actually were to have Annie in our lives until she was gone. It's like we were the guardians of a great and precious treasure. This huge responsibility was trying at times and required sacrifice and great commitment, primarily from my parents, but the honor and rewards of caring for someone so precious were tremendous. I always felt like I was special because I had a sister like Annie. I felt I had a secret glimpse into things other people could only guess at.

I always loved Annie, but I never realized how much happiness she gave me until she was gone. I always thought about trying to make her happy, to make her smile, and I didn't notice that it truly went both ways. I miss my little sister who I could always count on to be excited to see me. I miss her smile.

A couple of weeks after Annie died, I took my parents up to Piqua to visit Annie's gravesite and to see my grandma. At the cemetery, I sprinkled pink and yellow rose petals over Annie's grave where in a coffin below the earth her body lies dressed in a pale pink gown and covered with a rainbow afghan. An opal ring adorns her right hand and a delicate gold bracelet decorates her wrist. A toy hand mirror lies within reach above her hand.

For a while after Annie died, I woke up every morning with tears streaming down my face. After a while it was only every now and then. After six months that no longer happened, but it still hurt to think about her. I promised her I would look for her everywhere. And I did look, but I didn't see her; I couldn't feel her.

For a long time I struggled with how to think of Annie, or how to remember her. I wanted to believe she was freed from the constraints of this life and was perfect in every way. I didn't want to remember her in her crippled little body. I wanted her to be free from that, and I wanted my memories of her to be joyful in her new life and not carry the taint of sorrow at her condition in the life she left behind. But I struggled to visualize her in any way other than how I knew her. So in some ways, even the memory of her felt ethereal and lost to me.

Annie's wheelchair sat at the foot of her bed for nearly a year. And then one day my mom moved it out to the garage and covered it with plastic. The photo posters Carol and I made for the funeral still decorate Annie's room.

Carol said that after Annie's funeral she started to have some odd experiences in her room at night. She felt a presence, as if someone was standing there, always in the same corner of her room. She said usually when that happens she does some energy clearing to insist that the "spirit" leave. This time that didn't work. Finally after a few nights it occurred to her that maybe it was Annie visiting her and trying to get her attention. She opened to the possibility that it was Annie, and she asked for a sign if it was her. Carol felt like the spirit came over to where she was sitting and started jumping on the bed. Then she heard, "Let's dance."

Although I struggled at first about how to think of Annie after she died, now I can remember her as she was and find comfort in that. I remember her smiling at me, or being excited when I visited, and it makes me feel happy.

Every now and then I see a dove take flight, or a formation of geese float across the sky, or a soft and silent snowfall illuminated by my porch light in the black of the night, and I think of Annie. And sometimes, when all the pieces of my life fall easily into place, I wonder if she had a hand in it, and that makes me smile.

I look at the picture sitting on the table beside my computer desk of Annie smiling, as I write this last chapter. It feels like she is smiling at me and I think, You're happy I'm writing your story, aren't you Annie?

Sometimes in quiet moments, I like to close my eyes and imagine a circular clearing in a verdant green woods, ringed by sturdy oak trees that reach towards a brilliant blue sky. In the clearing, cheerful white daisies sway on their stems, and in the center a young woman dances to music that plays across the air. She is thin, small in stature, and is wearing a bright pink leotard underneath a filmy flowing skirt. Her long luxurious chestnut hair flows in waves down her back. She spins and her hair swirls around her head. She leaps and it streams behind her. Around and around, across the clearing, the dancer moves with joyous abandon. Her graceful motion fills the space. The dancer slows to a stop facing me, her deep brown eyes search mine, and then she flashes her smile.

Annie always was generous with her smiles.

When we've been here ten thousand years
Bright shining as the sun,

We've no less days to sing God's praise
Than when we've first begun.

ABOUT THE AUTHOR

Christine M. Grote earned a bachelor's degree in Chemical Engineering from the University of Dayton, Ohio, in 1979. After working for three and a half years in product development at Procter and Gamble in Cincinnati, Ohio, she became a full-time homemaker as she raised three sons and a daughter. In 1999, she returned to school at the College of Mount St. Joseph, Cincinnati, Ohio, earning a bachelor's degree in English in 2007.

Christine lives in Cincinnati, Ohio with her husband Mark and their dog Arthur.

CPSIA information can be obtained
at www.ICGtesting.com
Printed in the USA
LVHW04s1402160918
590319LV00011B/474/P